From Zero to Digital Hero

Discovering Opportunities, Navigating Challenges, and Launching a Successful Online Business for Absolute Beginners

Nolan Stafford

Summary

Chapter 1: Embarking on the Digital Journey

Welcome to the first chapter of this exciting book, where we will embark on an incredible journey into the world of digital technology! In this digital age, technology has become an inseparable part of our daily lives, revolutionizing the way we live, work, and interact with the world around us. In this chapter, we will explore the origins of the digital revolution, examine its impact on various aspects of our lives, and discuss the endless possibilities that lie ahead as we continue this remarkable journey.

1.1 The Dawn of the Digital Era

The roots of the digital revolution can be traced back to the late 20th century when a series of technological advancements brought forth the era of digitalization. One of the most noteworthy innovations during this time was the development of the microprocessor, a tiny integrated circuit that became the building block of modern computers. With the birth of the microprocessor, the stage was set for the digital transformation that would soon sweep across the globe.

The digital revolution gained significant traction in the 1980s, marked by the advent of personal computers. These compact machines allowed individuals to have computing power at their fingertips, enabling them to perform various tasks that were previously inconceivable. The proliferation of personal computers also paved the way for the emergence of the internet, a global network of interconnected computers that forever changed the way we communicate and access information.

1.2 Transforming Industries and Business Models

As the digital revolution continued to unfold, it had a profound impact on industries and business models worldwide. One of the sectors that experienced a radical transformation was the media and entertainment industry. The advent of digital technology disrupted traditional distribution channels, making way for streaming services that provide on-demand access to an unprecedented amount of content. Today, we can watch movies, listen to music, and read books from the comfort of our own homes, thanks to digital platforms like Netflix, Spotify, and Amazon Kindle.

The retail industry also felt the tremors of the digital revolution with the rise of e-commerce. Online shopping has forever changed the way we purchase goods, making it more convenient for consumers to find products, compare prices, and have items delivered directly to their doorsteps. From global giants like Amazon and Alibaba to local boutiques with online stores, e-commerce has democratized access to markets and fundamentally reshaped the retail landscape.

Furthermore, the digital revolution has empowered individuals to become entrepreneurs and create new business models. With the rise of social media platforms and online marketplaces, anyone with a unique idea or a product can build an online brand and reach a global audience. This has given rise to the gig economy, where individuals can offer their skills and services through digital platforms like Uber, Upwork, or Etsy, establishing a new paradigm for work and income generation.

1.3 Impact on Communication and Social Interactions

One of the most significant ways in which the digital revolution has transformed our lives is through communication and social interactions. The advent of the internet and social media platforms has made the world a smaller and more connected place. We can now communicate instantly with friends and family across the globe, share our thoughts and experiences with a diverse audience, and bridge cultural barriers through the click of a button.

Social media platforms like Facebook, Twitter, and Instagram have become virtual communities, enabling us to connect with like-minded individuals, discover new ideas, and stay informed about current events. They have also become powerful tools for activism and social change, allowing individuals to come together and rally for causes they believe in.

However, along with the positive impact, the digital revolution has also brought certain challenges to our social interactions. The rise of social media addiction and the constant need for validation through likes and comments have raised concerns about our mental health and the authenticity of our relationships. Striking a healthy balance between our online and offline lives is now more important than ever.

1.4 Education in the Digital Age

Education is yet another domain that has been profoundly influenced by the digital revolution. Traditional models of learning, confined to physical classrooms and textbooks, have been complemented and in some cases replaced by digital tools and platforms. Online courses, digital textbooks, and interactive learning applications have transformed the way we acquire knowledge and develop new skills. The digital era has democratized access to education, allowing individuals from various backgrounds to access quality learning materials at their own pace. Massive Open Online Courses (MOOCs) offered by platforms like Coursera, Udemy, and Khan Academy have provided millions of learners around the world with opportunities to explore diverse subjects and gain valuable certifications without the barriers of time and distance.

Moreover, the digital revolution has paved the way for personalized learning experiences, as artificial intelligence (AI) and machine learning algorithms can now adapt educational content to match individual student needs. The potential for AI in education is boundless, as it can help identify knowledge gaps, offer personalized feedback, and revolutionize the assessment process, ensuring a more effective and tailored learning experience for students worldwide.

1.5 The Future of Digitalization

As we conclude this first chapter of our digital journey, it is evident that the digital revolution has had a profound impact on various aspects of our lives. From transforming industries and business models to reshaping communication and education, we are witnessing the dawn of a new era that holds immense potential for the future.

Emerging technologies like artificial intelligence, blockchain, and the Internet of Things (IoT) are set to unleash even greater possibilities in the digital realm. These technologies have the potential to revolutionize healthcare, transportation, energy, and various other sectors, paving the way for a smarter, more connected, and sustainable world.

However, as we embark on this digital journey, it is crucial to navigate the challenges that lie ahead. Ethical considerations, data privacy, and digital inclusivity must be addressed as we navigate this rapidly evolving landscape.

In the upcoming chapters, we will delve deeper into specific aspects of the digital revolution, exploring emerging technologies, their impact on various industries, and the ethical considerations they bring forth. So fasten your seatbelts as we continue this exhilarating journey, exploring the ever-expanding horizons of the digital age.

The Digital Business Landscape

In today's fast-paced and interconnected world, the digital landscape has become an integral part of doing business. As technology continues to advance at an unprecedented rate, businesses must adapt and embrace digital strategies to stay competitive. The purpose of this chapter is to explore the various aspects of the digital business landscape, provide an overview of its significance, and highlight the opportunities and challenges it presents.

1.1.1 The Rise of Digital Transformation:

Digital transformation, the integration of digital technology into all areas of a business, has gained significant prominence in recent years. As consumers increasingly rely on digital platforms for their needs, businesses are compelled to enhance their digital presence to reach and engage their target audience effectively. The widespread availability of high-speed internet, coupled with the popularity of smartphones, has fueled this transformation, making the digital landscape a thriving ecosystem.

1.1.2 Shifting Consumer Behavior:

One of the key drivers of the digital business landscape is the shift in consumer behavior. The rise of e-commerce and online shopping has revolutionized the way people shop, making it more convenient and accessible. Consumers now expect businesses to provide seamless online experiences, personalized recommendations, and effortless transactions. Consequently, businesses must invest in technologies such as artificial intelligence and machine learning to capture and analyze consumer data to deliver tailored solutions.

Furthermore, social media platforms have become major influencers in shaping consumer decisions. Companies that leverage social media effectively can create brand awareness, engage with their audience, and build long-lasting relationships. Thus, businesses must understand and adapt to these changing consumer behaviors to thrive in the digital business landscape.

1.1.3 Digital Disruption:

Digital disruption refers to the phenomenon where innovative technologies disrupt existing business models, fundamentally changing the way industries operate. Established companies may find it challenging to adapt to these disruptions, while new startups leveraging digital technologies can rapidly gain market share. Familiar examples of digital disruption include Netflix, which disrupted the traditional video rental industry, and Uber, which transformed the transportation industry. Therefore, businesses must constantly innovate and embrace emerging technologies to stay relevant and avoid becoming victims of digital disruption.

1.1.4 Big Data and Analytics:

The digital business landscape generates an enormous amount of data every second. This data, commonly known as "big data," holds tremendous value for businesses. Big data analytics allows companies to gain insights into customer behavior, preferences, and trends. By harnessing the power of analytics, businesses can make data-driven decisions, identify growth opportunities, and create more targeted marketing campaigns.

However, handling and analyzing big data comes with its own set of challenges. Companies must invest in robust data infrastructure, ensure data privacy, and develop the necessary skills to extract meaningful insights. Additionally, companies need to strike a balance between utilizing customer data while respecting privacy concerns to build trust and maintain a positive reputation.

1.1.5 Cybersecurity:

As businesses increasingly operate in the digital realm, protecting sensitive data and safeguarding against cyber threats becomes imperative. Cybersecurity encompasses measures taken to prevent unauthorized access, theft, or damage to computers, networks, and data. The digital business landscape is prone to various cybersecurity risks, including data breaches, malware attacks, and phishing scams.

Businesses must invest in robust cybersecurity systems, regularly update software, and educate employees about best practices to mitigate these risks. Implementing appropriate security measures not only protects valuable assets but also builds trust with customers, creating a positive brand image.

1.1.6 E-Commerce and Omni-Channel Strategies:

E-commerce has grown exponentially over the years, presenting businesses with immense opportunities to optimize sales and expand their customer base. The digital business landscape enables companies to establish online stores, offering customers convenience, wide product selections, and hassle-free transactions. However, competition is fierce, and companies must differentiate themselves to succeed in this crowded market.

Omni-channel strategies have emerged as a potential solution for businesses to stand out in the digital landscape. With omni-channel, companies provide a seamless and integrated shopping experience across various platforms, including physical stores, websites, social media, and mobile apps. By blending the best of online and offline shopping, businesses can engage customers at multiple touchpoints, ensuring a consistent and personalized experience.

1.1.7 Artificial Intelligence and Automation:

Artificial Intelligence (AI) and automation technologies have the potential to revolutionize the digital business landscape. AI enables machines to mimic human intelligence, automating routine tasks, performing complex analyses, and increasing efficiency. Chatbots, for example, can enhance customer service by handling inquiries and resolving issues round the clock.

Automation also facilitates data processing, inventory management, and supply chain optimization, streamlining business operations. However, the integration of AI and automation requires careful planning to ensure a smooth transition and avoid unexpected consequences. Companies must assess the implications on transparency, ethics, and workforce implications while harnessing the power of these technologies.

1.1.8 The Gig Economy:

The digital business landscape has catalyzed the gig economy, where freelancers and independent contractors offer their skills and services on a short-term basis. Digital platforms such as Upwork and Freelancer have facilitated the growth of the gig economy, creating opportunities for individuals seeking flexible work arrangements.

Businesses can leverage the gig economy to access a diverse pool of talent, reduce overhead costs, and scale their operations according to demand. However, managing a distributed workforce comes with its own set of challenges, such as coordination, communication, and quality control. Companies should carefully navigate these challenges to fully capitalize on the potential advantages of the gig economy.

The digital business landscape is a dynamic and ever-evolving ecosystem that presents unparalleled opportunities and challenges for businesses.

To succeed in this rapidly changing world, companies must embrace digital transformation, understand changing consumer behaviors, and adapt their strategies accordingly.

Leveraging technologies like big data analytics, AI, and automation can unlock immense potential, while ensuring robust cybersecurity measures is paramount to protect valuable assets. By embracing the digital landscape, businesses can thrive in this digitally-driven era and remain competitive in the global marketplace.

The Power of Online Entrepreneurship

In today's rapidly evolving digital landscape, online entrepreneurship has emerged as a force to be reckoned with. It has revolutionized the traditional business models, turning individuals into successful entrepreneurs, and empowering them to chart their own paths towards financial independence and creative fulfillment.

The power of online entrepreneurship lies in its ability to transcend geographical boundaries, connecting entrepreneurs with a global audience. Through the power of the internet, entrepreneurs can reach potential customers, clients, and partners across the globe, irrespective of distance or time zones. This level of connectivity has transformed the possibilities available to budding entrepreneurs, opening up a world of opportunities.

One of the most significant advantages of online entrepreneurship is the ability to start with minimal financial investment. Gone are the days when launching a business required substantial capital, commercial real estate, or expensive equipment. Today, all an aspiring entrepreneur needs is an internet connection, a computer, and a brilliant idea. With these essentials in place, anyone can create their own online presence, build a website, and start offering products or services to a worldwide audience. This low barrier to entry is a game-changer, as it encourages innovation and creativity, leveling the playing field for entrepreneurs regardless of their financial background.

The internet serves as a vast marketplace where millions of transactions occur daily, constituting a potential goldmine for online entrepreneurs. E-commerce platforms provide entrepreneurs with an unparalleled opportunity to showcase and sell their products or services to an ever-expanding customer base. With the right marketing strategies and a compelling value proposition, entrepreneurs can attract customers from around the world, opening doors to exponential growth and profitability. Moreover, online platforms allow entrepreneurs to collect and analyze valuable customer data, enabling them to personalize their offerings and enhance customer experiences, fostering loyalty and driving customer retention.

Another aspect that makes online entrepreneurship so powerful is the scalability it offers. Traditional brick-and-mortar businesses are often limited by physical constraints. Expansion requires significant investment, additional locations, and a more extensive workforce. In contrast, online businesses can scale rapidly and efficiently, without the need for substantial physical infrastructure. With a few clicks of a button, entrepreneurs can increase their reach, offer new products or services, and serve a larger audience. Additionally, automation and outsourcing opportunities make it easier than ever before to handle increased demand without compromising quality. This scalability is a key advantage, as it allows online entrepreneurs to leverage their initial success and grow their businesses exponentially.

Online entrepreneurship also provides immense flexibility and freedom for individuals seeking a fulfilling work-life balance. The traditional nine-to-five grind can often be draining and restrictive. Online entrepreneurs have the liberty to set their own schedules, work from anywhere in the world, and pursue their passions. This freedom allows them to design a lifestyle that aligns with their personal values and priorities. Moreover, online entrepreneurship can eliminate many of the geographical limitations that traditional businesses face, allowing entrepreneurs to live in a location that provides them with the best quality of life or proximity to resources relevant to their industry.

One of the most remarkable aspects of online entrepreneurship is its capacity to foster collaboration and knowledge sharing. Online communities, forums, and platforms have become a hub for entrepreneurs to connect, learn, and seek guidance from like-minded individuals. This sense of community transcends borders, providing entrepreneurs with an extensive network of peers, mentors, and potential collaborators. The ability to tap into collective wisdom and experiences through these connections is invaluable, enabling entrepreneurs to navigate challenges more effectively, learn from others' mistakes, and accelerate their growth.

However, online entrepreneurship isn't without its challenges and risks. One of the major obstacles entrepreneurs face is the sheer volume of competition in the online space. With low barriers to entry, anyone can become an online entrepreneur, resulting in a crowded marketplace. To stand out, entrepreneurs need to differentiate their offerings, build a strong brand, and implement effective marketing strategies. Moreover, they must stay abreast of the latest trends, adapt to evolving customer demands, and constantly innovate to stay relevant in a highly dynamic digital landscape.

Security concerns and cyber threats also pose significant risks for online entrepreneurs. With the increasing reliance on technology, there is a heightened vulnerability to data breaches, hacking attempts, and other cybercrimes. Entrepreneurs need to invest in robust cybersecurity measures to protect their businesses and customer information. Failure to address these risks adequately can have severe consequences, including financial loss, reputational damage, and legal ramifications.

Online entrepreneurship holds immense potential for individuals seeking financial independence, creative fulfillment, and a flexible lifestyle. The power of online entrepreneurship lies in its ability to transcend geographical boundaries, provide low barriers to entry, offer scalability and automation opportunities, and foster a sense of community. Successful online entrepreneurs understand the challenges and risks involved and work diligently to differentiate themselves, build strong brands, and protect their businesses. With the right mindset, skillset, and a relentless drive for innovation, anyone can harness the power of online entrepreneurship and embark on a rewarding journey of self-empowerment and success.

Setting the Stage for Success

In every journey towards success, setting the stage plays a crucial role. Just like a play needs a well-prepared stage to captivate an audience, achieving our goals requires intentional planning and preparation. This chapter will explore the importance of setting the stage for success and provide actionable steps to take along the way.

Understanding the Purpose:

To embark on any meaningful endeavor, clarity of purpose is paramount. Before setting the stage for success, it is crucial to identify and define your goals or aspirations. This introspective process allows you to gain a deeper understanding of what you truly want to achieve, setting the foundation for the actions to follow.

Setting Realistic Goals:

Goals are the milestones that guide us towards our intended destination. However, it is essential to set realistic and achievable goals rather than aiming for the impossible. Unrealistic goals tend to breed frustration and disappointment, hindering our progress. By setting attainable targets, we can maintain motivation and momentum throughout the journey.

Creating a Vision:

A vision serves as a guiding light, casting a clear image of what success looks like. When setting the stage for success, it is vital to create a vivid vision of the desired outcome. This vision acts as a source of inspiration, reminding us why we started the journey and helping us stay on track during challenging times. Let your imagination roam freely and visualize yourself basking in the glory of accomplishing your goals.

Developing a Plan:

A well-structured plan is the roadmap that guides us towards success. It provides a framework for action, breaking down our goals into actionable steps. Without a plan, we risk becoming lost or overwhelmed along the way. Consider creating a timeline, setting measurable targets, and identifying key milestones to mark your progress. A plan should be dynamic, allowing for adjustments as new opportunities or challenges arise.

Building a Support Network:

No one achieves success in isolation. To set the stage for success, surround yourself with a supportive network of like-minded individuals who can provide guidance, encouragement, and accountability. Engaging with mentors, joining communities, and seeking out individuals who have already walked a similar path can significantly enhance your chances of success. Remember, collaboration and shared knowledge are powerful tools on the journey towards achievement.

Overcoming Obstacles:

Success is rarely a smooth journey devoid of obstacles and setbacks. However, it is our ability to overcome these challenges that sets us apart. Recognize that obstacles are an inherent part of the process and be prepared to face them head-on. Develop a growth mindset that views setbacks as opportunities for learning and self-improvement. By reframing challenges as stepping stones, you can navigate through them with resilience, adaptability, and determination.

Embracing Failure:

Failure is a stepping stone towards success, rather than an end in itself. Whether it is a setback or a mistake, failing provides invaluable lessons that fuel personal growth. Embrace failure as an opportunity to learn, recalibrate, and improve your approach. Each failure brings you closer to success by illuminating the path that doesn't lead to your desired outcome. As Thomas Edison said, "I have not failed. I've just found 10,000 ways that won't work."

Cultivating a Positive Mindset:

Success is often the result of a positive and resilient mindset. Nurturing a positive mental attitude allows you to approach challenges with optimism, persevere during difficult times, and capitalize on opportunities. Surround yourself with positivity by practicing gratitude, visualizing success, and maintaining a growth mindset. Believe in your capabilities and cultivate an unwavering belief in your ability to achieve greatness.

Taking Action:

Intention without action is merely a wish. To set the stage for success, it is vital to take consistent, purposeful action towards your goals. Break down your plan into manageable tasks and commit to executing them. Procrastination and hesitancy are the enemies of progress. By consistently taking action, you build momentum, reinforce positive habits, and inch closer to your desired destination. Setting the stage for success requires dedication, self-reflection, and deliberate action. It is a process that demands time, effort, and perseverance. By understanding your purpose, setting realistic goals, creating a vision, developing a plan, and building a support network, you lay a strong foundation for success. Embracing obstacles and failures along the way, cultivating a positive mindset, and consistently taking action complete the picture. Remember, the journey towards success is not a solitary endeavor but rather a symphony of deliberate choices, growth, and transformation.

Chapter 2: Building the Foundation

In our journey towards achieving our goals and dreams, it is crucial to lay a solid foundation. Just like a house needs a strong base to stand tall, our aspirations also require a sturdy groundwork that can support and sustain us throughout the challenging times. In this chapter, we will explore the significance of building a solid foundation and how it paves the way for our success.

1. Defining Success

Before we dive into the process of constructing a foundation, we must first define what success truly means to us. Success is a subjective concept, and it varies from person to person. For some, success may be financial stability, while for others, it may be maintaining a healthy work-life balance. Take the time to reflect on your personal values and aspirations to determine what success looks like for you. This self-reflection will serve as the compass guiding you towards building a foundation aligned with your goals.

2. Identifying Core Values

Our core values act as the building blocks of our foundation. They reflect our beliefs and principles, guiding every decision we make. It is essential to identify and prioritize our core values as they are the pillars that define our character and shape our journey. Take a moment to explore what matters most to you in life. Is it integrity, compassion, or personal growth? Pinpoint those core values that resonate deeply with you, for they will provide the strength and stability needed during challenging times.

3. Cultivating Self-Awareness

As we embark on building a foundation, it becomes crucial to develop a deep sense of self-awareness. Understanding our strengths, weaknesses, passions, and fears allows us to make informed choices and stay true to our path. Engage in regular self-reflection and introspection to gain a clear understanding of who you are and what you want to accomplish. Self-awareness is an ongoing process, a lifelong journey of discovery and growth.

4. Setting Clear Goals

Goals provide a sense of direction and purpose, acting as the blueprints for our foundation. To build a strong base, it is necessary to set clear and specific goals that are both challenging and attainable. Break down your larger aspirations into smaller, manageable steps, enabling you to make tangible progress. Remember to set goals that are aligned with your core values and aspirations, ensuring that each step you take is a step towards your personalized definition of success.

5. The Power of Discipline and Consistency

Building a foundation demands discipline and consistency. Success rarely occurs by chance or luck; instead, it is a result of deliberate action taken consistently over time. Develop daily habits and routines that support your goals and help you stay on track. It may be waking up early to work on your passion project or dedicating a specific amount of time each day for learning and personal growth. By embracing discipline and consistency, you create a sturdy framework for your foundation to thrive.

6. Embracing Failure and Resilience

In the process of building a foundation, failures and setbacks are inevitable. However, it is these very challenges that shape us and build our resilience. Embrace failure as an opportunity for growth and learning, rather than a sign of defeat. Remember that setbacks do not define your journey; it is how you bounce back that truly matters. Cultivating resilience allows you to navigate obstacles with grace and determination, ultimately strengthening the foundation you are building.

7. Seeking Support and Building Connections

No foundation is built in isolation. Surround yourself with individuals who support and inspire you on your journey. Seek mentors and role models who can provide guidance and wisdom. Building connections and nurturing relationships is not only beneficial for personal growth but also opens doors to opportunities. Collaboration and support from others contribute significantly to the foundation you are constructing, providing added strength and resilience.

8. Continuous Learning and Adaptability

A strong foundation relies on continuous learning and adaptability. Embrace a growth mindset that encourages continuous improvement and a willingness to evolve. Seek out new knowledge, skills, and experiences that align with your goals. Be open to change and adaptable in the face of unexpected circumstances. By committing to lifelong learning and adaptability, you ensure that your foundation remains sturdy and capable of withstanding even the most challenging storms.

9. Practicing Gratitude and Mindfulness

Gratitude and mindfulness play a vital role in building a solid foundation. Each day, take the time to reflect on the things you are grateful for, the progress you have made, and the lessons you have learned. Embrace mindfulness practices that help you stay present and grounded. By cultivating gratitude and living mindfully, you enhance your overall well-being and strengthen the foundation upon which you build your success.

Identifying Your Passion and Purpose

In the journey of life, finding our true passion and purpose is often considered one of the most essential and fulfilling aspects of our existence. It is the driving force behind our dreams, aspirations, and the ultimate path leading us towards personal fulfillment and success. Many individuals, however, struggle to pinpoint their passion and purpose, often feeling lost or disconnected from their true selves. But fear not, for this chapter aims to guide you on a profound exploration of yourself, helping you uncover your passions and purposes along the way.

The Essence of Passion

Passion is a powerful emotion that ignites an intense enthusiasm and eagerness within us. It is the spark that lights up our souls, fueling our desires, and propelling us towards meaningful endeavors. Identifying your passion requires a deep understanding of yourself, your interests, and what truly brings you joy. It transcends the boundaries of societal expectations and allows you to connect with your authentic self.

Discovering Your Passions

To embark on the journey of discovering your passions, it is crucial to engage in self-reflection and introspection. Start by asking yourself thought-provoking questions, such as:

1. What activities make you lose track of time?
2. What brings you immense joy and fulfillment?
3. What topics or subjects do you find yourself constantly seeking information about?
4. What skills or talents do others recognize in you?

As you ponder these questions, pay attention to the emotions and sensations that arise within you. Take note of the experiences and activities that resonate deeply, leaving you feeling invigorated and inspired. These moments of clarity are often clues that will guide you towards your passion.

Embracing Multiple Passions

It is important to note that passions are not always singular; they can encompass a variety of interests and pursuits. Some individuals are fortunate enough to have a clear and specific passion, while others may find joy in multiple endeavors. Embracing and exploring multiple passions is an enriching experience that adds depth to our lives. Rather than feeling overwhelmed by diverse interests, acknowledge them as part of your unique makeup and use them as fuel to create a harmonious blend of activities.

Purpose: The Soul's Calling

While passion ignites our desires, purpose gives us direction and meaning. Purpose stems from a profound understanding of ourselves and our place in the world, often linked to making a positive impact on others or society as a whole. Discovering your purpose requires delving into the depths of your values, beliefs, and aspirations.

Unveiling Your Purpose

The journey towards discovering your purpose can be an introspective and soul-searching process. Consider the following steps as signposts on this path:

1. Reflect on your values: Identify the core principles and beliefs that guide your actions and decision-making process. What deeply matters to you? What do you stand for?

2. Assess your strengths and skills: Recognize your natural abilities and the talents that come effortlessly to you. Reflect on how you can utilize these strengths to contribute to the lives of others.

3. Seek inspiration: Draw inspiration from people, causes, or situations that resonate with your values and passions. Explore the work of role models who have made a positive impact in areas you are passionate about, and analyze how their purpose aligns with

your own.

4. Follow your heart: Listen to your intuition, for it is often the voice of wisdom guiding you towards your purpose. Pay attention to the activities or causes that bring you a profound sense of joy, fulfillment, and meaning.

Connecting Passion and Purpose

Once you have identified your passions and purpose separately, the next step is to connect them. Finding the intersection between your passions and purpose allows you to create a life that is both fulfilling and meaningful. Consider how your passions can be channeled towards serving a greater purpose. How can your unique set of skills and interests contribute to the betterment of others or make a positive impact on the world?

Aligning with Your Authentic Self

As you embark on the journey of aligning with your passion and purpose, it is essential to connect with and embrace your authentic self. Society often imposes expectations and norms upon us, veiling our true passions and purposes. Embrace your uniqueness, celebrate your quirks, and allow your authentic self to guide you towards a life that resonates deeply with who you truly are.

Embracing the Journey

Discovering your passion and purpose is not an endpoint but rather a transformative journey that evolves and grows alongside you. Embrace the journey with an open heart and mind, remaining curious and adaptable.

Along the way, you may encounter obstacles, doubts, and moments of uncertainty, but remember that these are opportunities for growth and self-discovery.

Identifying your passion and purpose is a profound undertaking that requires self-reflection, introspection, and an open mind.

By embarking on this journey, you unlock the gateway to a life of fulfillment and aligning your actions with your truest self. Embrace your passions, follow your purpose, and delight in the harmony that unfolds when these elements intertwine.

May your journey towards self-discovery be one of immense joy, fulfillment, and authenticity.

Understanding Target Audiences and Niches

In today's competitive business landscape, it is essential for organizations to understand their target audiences and identify profitable niches. Whether you are a small startup or a well-established corporation, knowing your audience and catering to their needs is the key to success. This chapter delves into the intricacies of understanding target audiences and explores the significance of identifying and serving niches within your marketplace.

Section 1: Defining Target Audiences

Understanding the concept of a target audience is the first step towards effectively connecting with your customers. A target audience refers to a group of individuals who share common characteristics, interests, or purchasing behaviors. By identifying and understanding your target audience, you can focus your marketing efforts and resources more efficiently.

1.1 Demographics:

Demographic information plays a vital role in defining your target audience. These factors include age, gender, location, ethnicity, marital status, and household income. By analyzing demographic data, you can tailor your products, services, and marketing campaigns to cater specifically to your desired audience.

1.2 Psychographics:

Psychographics delve deeper into consumer behavior by evaluating attitudes, values, lifestyles, and motivations. Understanding the psychographics of your target audience allows you to create personalized marketing messages that resonate with their desires, aspirations, and preferences. For instance, an environmentally conscious target audience might respond more favorably to a sustainable product line.

1.3 Behavior:

Analyzing consumer behavior is critical for understanding how your target audience interacts with products and services. Behavior can include purchasing habits, brand loyalty, online engagement, and response to marketing efforts. By tracking these factors, you can modify your strategies, improve customer experiences, and increase conversion rates.

Section 2: Conducting Market Research

Once you have defined your target audience, conducting market research can provide invaluable insights into consumer needs and preferences. This research helps in identifying market trends, analyzing competitor strategies, and understanding the strengths and weaknesses of your own business.

2.1 Primary Research:

Primary research refers to collecting data firsthand through various methods such as surveys, interviews, and focus groups. This approach allows you to gather tailored information directly from your target audience, providing deeper insights and generating authentic responses.

2.2 Secondary Research:

Secondary research involves gathering existing data from reliable sources such as industry reports, government databases, and market intelligence platforms. This approach saves time and resources, as it provides a broader perspective on industry trends and consumer behaviors.

2.3 Competitive Analysis:

Analyzing competitors is crucial to understanding your industry landscape, identifying potential gaps, and differentiating your offerings. By examining their products, pricing, marketing strategies, and customer reviews, you can gain valuable knowledge to position yourself favorably in the market.

Section 3: Identifying Profitable Niches

Targeting a niche market involves catering to the specific needs and desires of a smaller, well-defined segment within your target audience. Identifying and serving these niches allows you to differentiate yourself from competitors and establish a loyal customer base.

3.1 Market Segmentation:

Market segmentation involves dividing your target audience into distinct groups based on shared characteristics or needs. By identifying unique segments, you can create tailored marketing messages and offerings that cater specifically to their requirements. This segmentation can be based on factors such as demographics, behavior, psychographics, or geography.

3.2 Niche Evaluation:

Once you have identified different market segments, the next step is to evaluate them for profitability and sustainability. Assessing factors such as size, growth potential, competition, and accessibility will help you prioritize and focus on the most viable niches.

3.3 Differentiation Strategy:

A differentiation strategy involves positioning your products or services uniquely within the chosen niche. This might include offering superior quality, unique features, exceptional customer service, or innovative solutions. By establishing a clear differentiator, you can attract and retain loyal customers within your niche.

Section 4: Implementation and Refinement

Understanding your target audience and identifying niches is only the beginning. The key to success lies in the implementation and continuous refinement of your strategies.

4.1 Targeted Marketing:

Armed with the insights gained from understanding your target audience, tailor your marketing efforts to reach them effectively. Utilize the most appropriate communication channels, create compelling content, and craft personalized messages that resonate with your audience's unique needs and desires.

4.2 Monitoring and Analytics:

Continuously monitor the performance of your marketing campaigns, track customer engagement metrics, and gather feedback. This data will provide valuable insights into the effectiveness of your strategies, allowing you to refine your approach and optimize your marketing efforts.

4.3 Evolution and Adaptation:

Consumer preferences and market dynamics evolve over time. It is crucial to stay abreast of industry trends, emerging technologies, and changing consumer demands.

By adapting and innovating, you can ensure long-term success and maintain a competitive edge within your target audience and niche. Understanding target audiences and identifying profitable niches is a relentless process that requires ongoing analysis, adaptation, and refinement. By comprehending the unique characteristics and needs of consumers, conducting thorough market research, and identifying viable niches, organizations can position themselves as industry leaders. Continuous implementation and evolution of strategies will enable businesses to thrive and create long-lasting relationships with their target audiences.

Crafting a Compelling Brand Identity

In today's competitive business landscape, establishing a strong brand identity is crucial for success. A compelling brand identity not only differentiates your business from competitors but also resonates with your target audience, creating a lasting impression. In this chapter, we will explore the various elements involved in crafting a compelling brand identity and how they contribute to building a strong brand.

Understanding Brand Identity:

Before delving into the process of crafting a brand identity, it's essential to understand what it truly entails. Brand identity refers to the collection of tangible and intangible attributes that define a brand and distinguish it from others. It encompasses everything from the visual representation of a brand, such as logos and color palettes, to the brand's values, mission, and personality.

1. Research and Analysis:

The first step in crafting a compelling brand identity is conducting thorough research and analysis. This involves gaining a deep understanding of your target audience, market trends, and competitors. By knowing your audience's preferences, demographics, and psychographics, you can tailor your brand identity to resonate with them effectively.

Additionally, analyzing market trends and competitors allows you to identify white spaces and unique selling propositions that can set your brand apart. Research can involve surveys, focus groups, competitor analysis, and industry trend tracking.

2. Define Your Brand's Personality:

Just like individuals, brands have personalities too. Defining your brand's personality is crucial as it helps shape all aspects of your communication and visual representation. Consider the characteristics and traits that best align with your brand. Is it bold and innovative? Or perhaps it leans towards being friendly and reliable? Understanding your brand's personality enables you to create a consistent tone of voice and visual style.

3. Develop Your Brand Positioning:

Brand positioning is about how your brand occupies a distinct spot in the minds of your target audience. It involves identifying your unique value proposition and clearly communicating it to your customers. Your brand positioning statement should clearly answer the question, "What sets your brand apart from competitors, and why should customers choose you?"

4. Visual Identity:

Visual elements play a significant role in creating a compelling brand identity. A well-designed logo, color scheme, typography, and visual assets can make a lasting impact on your audience. When developing your visual identity, consider the emotions and messages you want to convey. Choose colors and fonts that align with your brand's personality and reflect your target audience's preferences.

Moreover, consistency is key. Ensure that your visual elements are used consistently across all platforms and touchpoints, including your website, social media profiles, packaging, and marketing collateral. Consistency in visual identity builds brand recognition and strengthens the overall brand image.

5. Brand Storytelling:

In today's era of information overload, brand storytelling serves as a powerful tool to engage and connect with your audience. By crafting authentic, compelling stories, you can evoke emotions, build trust, and leave a lasting impression. Your brand story should communicate your values, purpose, and the journey that led to your establishment. It is a way to humanize your brand and build a connection with your audience.

6. Brand Voice and Messaging:

Consistency in brand voice and messaging is vital for creating a strong brand identity. Your brand voice should be reflective of your brand's personality and align with your target audience's preferences. Are you formal and professional, or casual and conversational? Determine the tone that best resonates with your audience and consistently apply it across all communication channels – from your website to social media posts.

7. Employee Alignment:

Your brand identity should not just be confined to external communication. It is equally important to ensure that your employees align with and embody your brand identity. Conduct internal brand workshops and training sessions to familiarize your team with the brand values, personality, and messaging. When employees fully understand and embrace the brand identity, they become brand ambassadors, delivering a consistent brand experience at every touchpoint.

8. Evolve and Adapt:

Creating a compelling brand identity doesn't mean it's set in stone forever. As your business evolves and adapts to changing market dynamics, your brand identity may need to be reviewed and refined. Regularly revisit and analyze your branding strategy, seeking feedback from customers and employees. This allows you to make necessary adjustments to keep your brand identity relevant and impactful.

Crafting a compelling brand identity is an ongoing journey that requires careful consideration and effort. By conducting thorough research, defining your brand's personality, designing a visual identity, telling authentic stories, and consistently communicating your brand voice, you can build a strong and resonant brand identity. Remember that brand identity is not stagnant – it should evolve and adapt as your business grows, allowing you to remain relevant and capture the hearts and minds of your target audience.

Establishing Your Online Presence

In today's digital era, building a strong online presence has become increasingly vital for individuals and businesses alike. Our lives are no longer confined to the physical world; instead, we share our interests, thoughts, and experiences through various online platforms. Whether you're a professional looking to enhance your career prospects or an entrepreneur aiming to promote your brand, establishing a robust online presence is the key to success.

This chapter delves into the fundamental aspects of establishing a compelling online presence. We'll explore the importance of personal branding, creating an engaging presence on social media, building a professional website, and optimizing your online activities. So, let's embark on this exciting journey and unlock the secrets to building a captivating presence in the digital realm.

1. Understanding Personal Branding

When crafting your online presence, it's essential to understand the concept of personal branding. Just like organizations and businesses have their unique brand identities, individuals can cultivate their personal brand. Personal branding encompasses the qualities, values, expertise, and image that you want to convey to the world. It's about authentically showcasing who you are, what you stand for, and what sets you apart from others.

To establish a strong personal brand online, start by identifying your strengths, passions, and unique selling points. Understand your target audience and tailor your content to resonate with them. Consistency is key when it comes to personal branding, so ensure your message aligns across different online platforms.

2. Developing an Engaging Social Media Presence

Social media has revolutionized the way we connect and communicate with others. It has emerged as a powerful tool for building an online presence. However, to leverage its potential, it's crucial to create an engaging social media presence that captivates your audience.

Start by choosing the platforms that best suit your personal or professional goals. Each platform caters to different demographics and content formats. Whether it's Facebook, Twitter, Instagram, LinkedIn, or even emerging platforms like TikTok, understanding the platform's dynamics is essential.

Craft a social media strategy that aligns with your personal brand and goals. Post regularly, but ensure your content is of high quality and brings value to your audience. Engage with your followers by responding to comments, asking questions, and participating in relevant conversations. Building authentic connections will help you foster a loyal and growing community.

3. Establishing a Professional Website

While social media plays a significant role in your online presence, having a dedicated website is equally crucial. A website serves as a central hub where people can learn more about you, your work, and your accomplishments. It provides a deeper dive into your expertise and allows you to showcase your portfolio, blog, or projects.

Start by choosing a domain name that reflects your personal brand or business. Ensure it's easy to remember and aligns with your online identity. Then, design a visually appealing and user-friendly website that reflects your brand's aesthetics. Use a content management system like WordPress or Squarespace to simplify the website creation process.

Your website should provide relevant information about your background, services, skills, or products. Incorporate a call-to-action to encourage visitors to connect with you or subscribe to your newsletter. Regularly update your website with fresh content, ensuring it stays relevant and engaging.

4. Optimizing Your Online Activities

To truly maximize your online presence, it's essential to optimize your online activities for search engines. Search Engine Optimization (SEO) is a practice that helps your content rank higher in search engine results, driving organic traffic to your website or social media profiles.

Keyword research is a crucial aspect of SEO. Understand the keywords your target audience is searching for and strategically incorporate them into your website copy, blog posts, social media bios, and content titles. This will increase the likelihood of search engines recognizing your content as authoritative and relevant.

Additionally, focus on creating valuable and shareable content that integrates seamlessly with your personal brand. Infographics, videos, or in-depth blog posts not only provide useful information but are more likely to be shared, expanding your reach and further solidifying your online presence.

Experiment with different types of content and monitor analytics to understand what resonates most with your audience. Adapt your strategy accordingly, consistently improving and optimizing your online activities.

Unlocking Your Online Potential

Establishing a captivating online presence requires time, dedication, and strategic planning. By understanding the importance of personal branding, developing an engaging social media presence, creating a professional website, and optimizing your online activities, you'll be able to unlock your full potential in the digital landscape.

Remember, building an online presence is an ongoing process. Continuously monitor trends, adapt to new platforms, and refine your strategy along the way.

Your digital footprint is an opportunity to showcase your talents, expertise, and passions to the world, so seize it with enthusiasm and confidence. Let your online presence shine and set yourself up for success in both your personal and professional endeavors!

Chapter 3: Cracking the Code of Online Success

In today's digital age, the quest for online success is a pursuit that has captivated entrepreneurs, marketers, and individuals alike. With the global landscape becoming increasingly interconnected, the online sphere has transformed into a battleground where businesses thrive or falter. As we delve into Chapter 3, we embark on a journey to unravel the secrets behind cracking the code of online success.

1. Navigating the Digital Landscape

Imagine stepping into a vast and mysterious labyrinth, where every turn holds new challenges and opportunities. This labyrinth is none other than the digital landscape, a complex and ever-changing world where success lies in deciphering the hidden code. To succeed online, it is crucial to understand the intricacies of this landscape.

At the heart of online success lies a fundamental rule: understanding your audience. Conducting thorough research to understand your target demographic, their preferences, and needs is the key to unlocking the potential of your online venture. By grasping the intricacies of your audience, you can tailor your strategies to resonate with them, creating a strong foundation for success.

2. Crafting Engaging Content

In the quest for online success, content is king. With billions of web pages and social media posts clamoring for attention, grabbing the spotlight requires creating engaging and captivating content. Whether it's a blog post, video, podcast, or social media update, the success of your online presence hinges on delivering value to your target audience.

When crafting content, quality and relevance are paramount. Gone are the days of generic and spam-like content. Authenticity and expertise are the cornerstones of effective content creation. By employing storytelling techniques, providing actionable advice, and addressing your audience's pain points, you can establish a strong connection, foster trust, and drive engagement.

3. The Power of Search Engine Optimization (SEO)

While creating compelling content is crucial, it is equally important to ensure your target audience can find it. This is where Search Engine Optimization (SEO) comes into play. SEO is the art and science of optimizing your online presence to rank higher on search engine result pages, enabling your content to be easily discovered by your target audience.

To crack the code of SEO success, understanding the underlying algorithms utilized by search engines such as Google and Bing is vital. By conducting extensive keyword research, optimizing on-page elements, and building high-quality backlinks, you can enhance your website's visibility and attract organic traffic. Staying up to date with the latest SEO trends and algorithms is a continuous endeavor, but one that is imperative for online success.

4. Embracing Social Media's Impact

In the digital era, social media has emerged as a formidable force, reshaping the ways businesses and individuals communicate, connect, and share information. Harnessing the power of social media is a crucial aspect of cracking the code of online success.

By identifying the social media channels that align with your audience's preferences, interests, and demographics, you can leverage these platforms to reach and engage with your target market. Crafting a coherent social media strategy involves creating captivating content, leveraging user-generated content, engaging with your audience, and utilizing data analytics to optimize your approach. Social media acts as a powerful tool in building brand awareness, driving traffic, and fostering customer loyalty.

5. Building a Trustworthy Online Reputation

With a multitude of choices available online, establishing a trustworthy reputation is essential for success. Building credibility and trust is a multifaceted process that requires consistency, authenticity, and delivering on promises. Businesses and individuals alike must invest in nurturing their online reputation to crack the code of online success.

One of the defining elements of a trustworthy reputation is customer reviews and testimonies. Positive reviews act as social proof, influencing a potential customer's decision-making process. Encouraging satisfied customers to leave reviews, providing exceptional customer service, and actively resolving any negative feedback are vital steps in building a positive online reputation.

6. The Evolution of Online Advertising

As the digital landscape has evolved, so too has the world of online advertising. Gone are the days when pop-up ads and obtrusive banners dominated the online sphere. Today, cracking the code of online success requires embracing innovative advertising strategies that seamlessly integrate with the user experience.

Investing in targeted advertising platforms such as Google Ads, Facebook Ads, and native advertising solutions can yield remarkable results. By utilizing data-driven insights, segmenting your audience, and crafting personalized and relevant ad campaigns, you can attract the right audience at the right time. Additionally, the rise of influencer marketing has opened up new avenues for businesses to connect with their target audience by leveraging the influence and credibility of online personalities.

7. Adapting to New Technologies

The digital landscape is never stagnant, constantly being shaped by emerging technologies. Staying ahead of the curve and adapting to new technologies is vital for cracking the code of online success. From artificial intelligence and chatbots to virtual reality and augmented reality, embracing these advancements can provide a competitive edge.

By leveraging chatbots, for example, businesses can deliver personalized support and streamline their customer service process. Virtual and augmented reality technologies enable immersive online experiences, revolutionizing industries such as e-commerce and marketing. Adapting to these new technologies allows businesses to enhance customer experiences, capture attention, and differentiate themselves in a crowded online space.

Cracking the code of online success requires a holistic approach that encompasses understanding your audience, crafting engaging content, optimizing for search engines, embracing social media, building trust, utilizing innovative advertising strategies, and adapting to emerging technologies. The digital landscape may appear daunting, but by unraveling its secrets and aligning your strategies, you can unlock the door to online success.

Navigating the World of E-Commerce

In the rapidly changing world of commerce, electronic commerce, or e-commerce, has emerged as a powerful force shaping the way we buy and sell goods and services. The convenience it offers has made it increasingly popular among both consumers and businesses. However, successfully navigating the world of e-commerce requires a nuanced understanding of its intricacies, challenges, and opportunities. This chapter aims to provide you with a comprehensive overview of e-commerce, enabling you to navigate this exciting and ever-evolving domain.

The Evolution of E-Commerce

E-commerce is not a recent phenomenon. Its roots can be traced back to the early 1970s when electronic data interchange (EDI) systems were developed to facilitate transactions between businesses. Over time, advancements in technology, especially the internet, revolutionized e-commerce, making it accessible to individuals worldwide. The first online shopping experiences emerged in the 1980s, gradually transforming into the vibrant e-commerce ecosystem we see today.

Understanding the E-Commerce Landscape

E-commerce encompasses a wide range of activities, including online retail (B2C), online wholesale (B2B), electronic payments, online auctions, and online marketplaces. Each of these subdomains offers unique challenges and opportunities. Let's explore some of the essential aspects of e-commerce in greater detail:

1. Online Retail (B2C): The consumer-facing aspect of e-commerce, B2C, has experienced exponential growth in recent years. A multitude of online platforms, such as Amazon, eBay, and Alibaba, have revolutionized the way people shop for goods and services. While traditional brick-and-mortar stores continue to thrive, online retail offers unparalleled convenience, variety, and often competitive pricing.

2. Online Wholesale (B2B): B2B e-commerce focuses on transactions between businesses. This segment caters to enterprises that require large quantities of goods or services. Digital marketplaces, such as Alibaba's business-to-business platform, have greatly simplified procurement processes for companies, fostering efficient global trade connections.

3. Electronic Payments: One of the fundamental aspects of e-commerce is secure electronic payments. Payment gateways, such as PayPal, Stripe, and Square, have become an essential part of online transactions, ensuring that financial information remains protected while allowing customers to make hassle-free purchases. The rapid rise of digital wallets, like Apple Pay and Google Pay, further streamlines the payment process.

4. Online Auctions: Auction websites, such as eBay, have created an entirely new realm of online buying and selling. Online auctions allow consumers to engage in bidding wars for rare or unique items, creating exciting and dynamic marketplaces. Additionally, businesses can also leverage online auctions to liquidate excess inventory or find potential buyers for specific items.

5. Online Marketplaces: Online marketplaces act as intermediaries, connecting buyers and sellers in a single platform. These platforms, such as Amazon, Shopify, and Etsy, offer sellers the opportunity to reach a broader audience and simplify the selling process. By handling various aspects like inventory management, order fulfillment, and customer service, online marketplaces have democratized e-commerce, enabling small businesses to thrive in a global marketplace.

Challenges and Opportunities in E-Commerce

E-commerce provides a world of possibilities, but it is not without its challenges. Here are a few key areas that both businesses and consumers should consider:

1. Trust and Security: One of the biggest concerns in e-commerce is trust. Consumers need assurance that their personal and financial information is secure, and businesses need to establish trust to attract and retain customers. Implementing robust security measures, using secure payment gateways, and obtaining SSL certificates are vital steps to ensure a safe online environment.

2. Logistics and Supply Chain Management: Effective supply chain management is critical for successful e-commerce operations. Businesses must master the art of inventory management, order fulfillment, and efficient product delivery. Optimization of logistics and careful selection of shipping partners are essential to provide customers with a seamless shopping experience.

3. Competition and Differentiation: As the e-commerce space becomes increasingly saturated, standing out from the competition is crucial. Businesses must invest in creating a unique brand identity

and building customer loyalty. Offering exceptional customer service, innovative marketing strategies, and personalized experiences can help differentiate a business in a crowded marketplace.

4. Mobile Commerce: The proliferation of smartphones and mobile internet has led to the rise of mobile commerce, or m-commerce. Businesses must adapt their websites and online platforms to be mobile-friendly to tap into the growing market of mobile users. Optimizing user experience, incorporating mobile payment solutions, and leveraging location-based services are key strategies for success in m-commerce.

E-commerce has transformed the way we buy and sell goods and services, offering convenience, accessibility, and a global marketplace to both consumers and businesses. This chapter aimed to provide you with an overview of the vast landscape of e-commerce, from understanding its evolution to exploring its various dimensions. By carefully considering the challenges and opportunities presented by e-commerce, businesses and consumers can navigate this ever-evolving domain successfully. With continued advancements in technology, e-commerce will undoubtedly shape the future of commerce, and it is imperative to always stay updated and adaptable in this dynamic digital era.

Unveiling the Secrets of Digital Marketing

In this digital age, where technology has become an integral part of our lives, businesses must adapt to new marketing strategies to stay ahead of the competition. Digital marketing has emerged as a powerful tool to reach and engage with potential customers, enabling businesses to connect with a global audience like never before. However, many entrepreneurs and marketers struggle with understanding the intricacies of digital marketing. In this chapter, we will explore the secrets behind successful digital marketing campaigns, unveiling the strategies and techniques used by industry experts to achieve outstanding results.

Understanding the Digital Landscape

Before diving into the secrets of digital marketing, it is crucial to understand the ever-evolving digital landscape. The internet, social media, search engines, and mobile devices have revolutionized the way businesses communicate with their target audience. To effectively utilize digital marketing, businesses must analyze consumer behavior, technological advancements, and industry trends.

One of the secrets to successful digital marketing is having a solid online presence. This involves creating a user-friendly website, implementing effective SEO techniques, and engaging on social media platforms. Having a strong presence allows businesses to establish credibility, build trust, and increase brand visibility in the digital realm.

Defining Objectives and Target Audience

Digital marketing is not a one-size-fits-all approach. Every business has unique goals and target audiences. To unveil the secrets of digital marketing, businesses must define their objectives and identify their ideal customer base. Setting specific, measurable, achievable, relevant, and time-bound (SMART) goals is crucial for a successful digital marketing campaign.

Understanding the target audience is equally important. Conducting market research, analyzing customer demographics, and studying online behaviors will provide valuable insights into consumer preferences. By uncovering the secrets of a specific target audience, businesses can tailor their digital marketing strategies to effectively reach and resonate with potential customers.

Content is King

In the realm of digital marketing, content is king. High-quality content is the foundation of any successful digital marketing campaign. It drives organic traffic, engages the audience, and establishes authority in the industry. Unveiling the secrets of content creation involves understanding the target audience's pain points, preferences, and interests.

Creating valuable and relevant content can take various forms such as blog posts, articles, videos, infographics, and podcasts. The key is to develop content that educates, entertains, or solves a problem for the audience. Content should be optimized for search engines, incorporating relevant keywords that align with the target audience's search intent.

Embracing Social Media

Another secret to successful digital marketing is harnessing the power of social media. Social media platforms have transformed into a playground for businesses to engage, interact, and convert potential customers. However, the key lies in understanding the nuances of each platform and tailoring content accordingly.

Different social media platforms serve different purposes. Facebook is ideal for building brand awareness, Twitter for real-time updates, Instagram for visual storytelling, and LinkedIn for professional networking. By identifying the platforms where the target audience spends the most time, businesses can craft targeted social media strategies to maximize engagement and conversions.

Search Engine Optimization (SEO)

At the core of digital marketing lies search engine optimization (SEO). SEO involves optimizing websites to rank higher in search engine results for specific keywords. Unveiling the secrets of SEO requires understanding on-page and off-page optimization techniques.

On-page SEO involves optimizing website content, meta tags, headings, images, and URLs to make it more search engine-friendly. Off-page SEO focuses on building backlinks, generating social signals, and increasing website authority. By mastering the art of SEO, businesses can drive organic traffic, improve visibility, and attract potential customers.

The Power of Influencer Marketing

Influencer marketing has emerged as a secret weapon for successful digital marketing campaigns. Influencers have a loyal and engaged following who trust their recommendations. Collaborating with influencers relevant to the industry can help businesses tap into their audience and gain credibility.

The key to unlocking the secrets of influencer marketing lies in finding the right influencers who align with the brand's values, target audience, and objectives. By leveraging influencer partnerships, businesses can expand their reach, drive conversions, and establish themselves as industry leaders.

Email Marketing Automation

Email marketing, when done right, can be a valuable asset for businesses. Utilizing email marketing automation tools is one of the secrets to success in digital marketing. Automation allows businesses to send personalized and targeted emails to potential customers at different stages of the customer journey.

Segmenting the email list based on demographics, behavior, and interactions is crucial for effective email marketing. Sending personalized emails at the right time can nurture leads, build customer loyalty, and drive conversions. Unveiling the secrets of email marketing automation involves continuously analyzing and optimizing campaigns based on data and feedback.

The Importance of Data Analysis

One of the secrets behind successful digital marketing is data analysis. In the digital realm, businesses have access to an abundance of data that can unveil insights and trends. Analyzing data helps businesses understand consumer behavior, identify marketing campaign performance, and make data-driven decisions.

Utilizing analytics tools such as Google Analytics provides businesses with valuable information about website traffic, conversions, bounce rates, and user behavior. By regularly analyzing data, businesses can uncover the secrets of what works and what doesn't, enabling them to refine their digital marketing strategies for optimal results.

In this chapter, we delved into the secrets of digital marketing, exploring the strategies and techniques used by industry experts to achieve outstanding results.

From understanding the digital landscape to embracing social media, SEO, influencer marketing, and data analysis, businesses can unlock the potential of digital marketing.

By applying these secrets, businesses can connect with their target audience, drive conversions, and thrive in the ever-evolving digital world.

Mastering Social Media Engagement

In today's digitally connected world, social media has become a vital tool for individuals, businesses, and organizations to engage and interact with their target audience. The power of social media cannot be underestimated. It provides an unprecedented opportunity to build brand awareness, create meaningful connections, and foster a loyal community. However, mastering social media engagement requires more than just posting content. It demands a deep understanding of the platforms, the target audience, and the ability to create compelling and interactive content. In this chapter, we will explore the key strategies and techniques to help you become a master of social media engagement.

Understanding Your Audience

Before diving into the world of social media engagement, it is essential to understand your audience inside out. Who are they? What are their interests? Where do they spend most of their time online? Conducting thorough market research and building detailed buyer personas will serve as the foundation for your social media engagement efforts. By understanding your audience's preferences, pain points, and motivations, you can tailor your content to resonate with them.

Choosing the Right Platforms

Social media platforms are not created equal, so it's crucial to select the ones that align with your brand and reach your target audience effectively. Facebook, Twitter, Instagram, LinkedIn, and TikTok are just a few of the platforms dominating today's social media landscape. Take the time to analyze which platforms your audience favors and invest your resources accordingly. It's better to excel on a few platforms than spread yourself too thin across multiple channels.

Creating Compelling Content

One of the primary drivers of successful social media engagement is creating and sharing high-quality content. Content that is engaging, informative, and visually appealing will capture the attention of your audience and encourage them to interact with your brand. Visual content, such as images and videos, tend to perform exceptionally well across various social media platforms. Embrace storytelling in your content and leverage emotions to create a connection with your audience. Remember, content should be both valuable and shareable to maximize engagement.

Encouraging User-generated Content

User-generated content (UGC) is a powerful tool to amplify your social media engagement efforts. It involves encouraging your audience to create and share content related to your brand, products, or services. UGC not only builds trust and authenticity but also fosters a sense of community around your brand. Contests, hashtags, and challenges are effective ways to spark UGC. Share and celebrate UGC to create a cycle where your audience feels appreciated and motivated to engage with your brand further.

Implementing a Conversational Approach

Gone are the days of one-sided communication on social media. To master social media engagement, adopt a conversational approach by actively listening and engaging with your audience. Be responsive to comments, messages, and mentions across all your social media platforms. Show genuine interest in what your audience has to say, and don't shy away from engaging in meaningful conversations. This humanizes your brand and fosters a stronger connection with your audience.

Leveraging Influencer Partnerships

In the world of social media, influencers hold tremendous sway over their followers. Collaborating with influencers who align with your brand's values and target audience can significantly boost your social media engagement. When partnering with influencers, ensure that they genuinely believe in your brand and are not just looking for monetary compensation. Authenticity is key to maintaining trust and credibility.

Using Data Analytics to Drive Engagement

To truly master social media engagement, you must embrace data analytics. Regularly monitor and analyze engagement metrics such as likes, comments, shares, and click-through rates. This data provides valuable insights into what content resonates with your audience and what doesn't. It allows you to make data-driven decisions to optimize your social media strategy continually. Experiment with different content formats, posting schedules, and hashtags to refine your approach and maximize engagement.

Staying Relevant and Adapting to Trends

The social media landscape is continuously evolving, and it's essential to stay ahead of the curve. Keep a close eye on emerging trends, features, and changes in algorithms across different platforms. Incorporate new features like Instagram Reels or Twitter Spaces into your strategy to keep your content fresh and engaging. Stay relevant by capitalizing on trending topics and participating in relevant conversations. Flexibility and adaptation are key to maintaining an engaging social media presence.

Building a Community

Building a loyal and engaged community around your brand is the ultimate goal of social media engagement. Encourage your audience to be active participants in discussions, share their thoughts, and feel like an integral part of your brand's journey. Create exclusive groups or communities on platforms like Facebook or LinkedIn to foster deeper connections and facilitate meaningful interactions between your brand and your audience. Engage with your community consistently and provide value to establish long-lasting relationships.

Mastering social media engagement is an ongoing process that requires patience, creativity, and a deep understanding of your audience and the platforms you use. By strategically selecting the right platforms, creating compelling content, leveraging user-generated content, embracing a conversational approach, partnering with influencers, utilizing data analytics, staying adaptable to trends, and building a community, you can elevate your social media engagement efforts to new heights. Remember, social media is not just about gaining likes and followers; it's about building authentic connections and fostering meaningful relationships with your audience.

Search Engine Optimization (SEO) Demystified

In today's digital landscape, where businesses are constantly striving to expand their online presence, search engine optimization (SEO) has become an essential tool for success. SEO involves various strategies and techniques that help websites rank higher on search engine result pages (SERPs), ultimately driving more organic traffic and increasing online visibility. This chapter will demystify the world of SEO, providing you with a comprehensive understanding of its key principles and practices.

1. What is SEO?

Search engine optimization (SEO) refers to the process of optimizing a website and its content to rank higher on search engine results based on specific keywords or phrases. The ultimate goal is to improve organic (non-paid) search engine visibility, attracting more relevant traffic to a website.

2. Why is SEO Important?

In the age of information overload, search engines serve as gatekeepers, connecting users to the most relevant and valuable content. Therefore, if your website does not appear on the first page of search results, it is unlikely to receive significant organic traffic. By investing in SEO, you can improve your website's visibility and increase its chances of being discovered by potential customers.

3. How Search Engines Work

Understanding how search engines function is crucial for effective SEO. Search engines, such as Google, Bing, and Yahoo, use complex algorithms to analyze and rank websites based on numerous factors. These algorithms constantly evolve, aiming to provide users with the most accurate and useful search results.

The ranking factors can be broadly categorized into:

3.1 On-Page Factors

On-page factors refer to elements that are under your direct control, such as content, meta tags, and URL structure. By optimizing these aspects, you can ensure search engines understand your website's relevance to specific queries.

- High-Quality Content: Creating unique, well-written, and engaging content is fundamental. Focus on providing valuable information that addresses users' needs.
- Keyword Optimization: Conduct thorough keyword research to identify relevant keywords and incorporate them into your content strategically. However, avoid keyword stuffing, as it may be seen as spammy by search engines.
- Meta Tags: Optimize your meta title and description tags, making them compelling and keyword-rich. These tags are displayed on SERPs and can increase your click-through rate.
- URL Structure: Use descriptive URLs that include relevant

keywords. These customized URLs are not only user-friendly but also help search engines understand the content of your pages.

- Image Optimization: Compress and optimize images to improve page load speed. Additionally, use alt tags to describe images, which helps search engines understand the visual content.

3.2 Off-Page Factors

Off-page factors are external signals that influence your website's visibility and authority. The primary off-page factor is backlinks – links from other websites pointing to yours. Search engines consider these links as endorsements, indicating the quality and relevance of your content.

- Link Building: Engage in ethical link-building practices to acquire high-quality backlinks. This can be achieved through guest posting, partnerships, social media promotion, and networking within your industry.
- Social Signals: Establish a strong presence on social media platforms to encourage social sharing and engagement. Popular content that receives numerous shares and comments can indirectly improve your SEO performance.
- Brand Mentions: Being mentioned by reputable websites or influencers can significantly enhance your website's authority. Monitor and engage with online mentions of your brand to leverage these opportunities.

3.3 Technical Factors

Technical factors pertain to the infrastructure and backend aspects of a website that impact its crawlability, indexability, and overall performance.

- Website Speed: Optimize your website's loading speed since search engines prioritize fast-loading sites. Compress images, minify CSS/JavaScript files, leverage caching mechanisms, and utilize content delivery networks (CDNs) to improve speed.
- Mobile-Friendliness: With the rise in mobile device usage, search engines prioritize mobile-friendly websites. Ensure your website is responsive and offers an optimal user experience across various screen sizes.
- Website Structure: Organize your website architecture in a logical and hierarchical manner to assist search engine crawlers in understanding the content's relevance and structure.
- XML Sitemap: Create and submit an XML sitemap to search engines. This file helps search engines to discover and index your web pages efficiently.

4. Staying Up-to-Date with SEO

The field of SEO is ever-evolving, with search engine algorithms frequently updating and introducing new ranking factors. To ensure long-term success, it is essential to stay informed about the latest SEO trends, techniques, and best practices.

- Industry News and Blogs: Regularly follow reputable industry news websites and blogs dedicated to SEO to stay informed about algorithm updates, case studies, and expert opinions.

- Webmaster Guidelines: Refer to the webmaster guidelines provided by search engines, such as Google's Webmaster Guidelines. These guidelines outline practices that can positively impact your website's visibility while steering clear of penalties.

- Continuous Learning and Experimentation: Attend SEO conferences, workshops, and webinars to gain insights from industry leaders. Additionally, constantly experiment with different strategies, monitor the results, and adapt accordingly.

SEO is a dynamic field that encompasses various strategies and techniques to improve a website's visibility on search engines. By optimizing on-page elements, building high-quality backlinks, and focusing on technical aspects, you can enhance your website's chances of ranking higher on search engine result pages. Remember, SEO requires an ongoing effort and adaptation to stay ahead of the curve, ensuring your website remains visible and attracts valuable organic traffic.

Chapter 4: From Idea to Action

Turning an idea into action is often the most challenging part of any endeavor. Every great accomplishment, from writing a book to launching a successful business, begins with a spark of inspiration. However, having an idea alone is not enough; it requires dedication, planning, and relentless pursuit to bring it to fruition. In this chapter, we will delve into the various stages involved in transforming an idea into action and explore the strategies and mindset necessary for success.

The Birth of an Idea:

Ideas are the seeds of innovation. They usually arise from a combination of observation, curiosity, and a desire to solve a problem. However, not all ideas are born equal. Some may be fleeting and lack substance, while others have the potential to change the world.

To determine the viability and potential of an idea, one must evaluate its feasibility, market demand, and uniqueness. Conducting thorough research on similar concepts, gathering feedback from potential users or consumers, and seeking expert opinions can aid in this evaluation process. Moreover, brainstorming sessions and engaging in discussions with like-minded individuals can help refine and polish the initial concept.

The Dreamer's Dilemma:

While ideas hold immense potential, the path from idea to action is often riddled with challenges and doubts. The dreamer's dilemma lies in the struggle to bridge the gap between imagination and reality. Fear of failure, self-doubt, and a multitude of distractions can hinder progress and drain motivation.

However, overcoming the dreamer's dilemma requires a shift in mindset. Realizing that failure is merely a stepping stone to success can be liberating. Embracing failure as an opportunity to learn, grow, and iterate upon ideas is crucial. Additionally, cultivating discipline, resilience, and perseverance can help navigate the obstacles that lie ahead.

Developing an Action Plan:

Once an idea has been refined and there is a firm resolve to move forward, developing an action plan becomes paramount. Breaking down the idea into smaller, manageable tasks enhances clarity and provides a roadmap for progress. Each task should have realistic deadlines and clear objectives, allowing for measurable milestones along the way.

Furthermore, creating a visual representation of the action plan, such as a Gantt chart or a Kanban board, helps track progress and ensures accountability. Allocating resources, whether financial, human, or time-related, is equally essential to enable the successful execution of the plan.

Building a Support Network:

No one ever achieves greatness alone. Building a strong support network is vital in turning an idea into action. Surrounding oneself with like-minded individuals who believe in the vision can provide encouragement, moral support, and valuable input.

Seeking out mentors and experts in relevant fields can also prove invaluable. Their wisdom and guidance can help refine ideas further, provide insights into potential pitfalls, and open doors to new opportunities. Additionally, networking and actively participating in relevant communities can lead to collaborations and partnerships that can accelerate progress.

Executing with Passion and Purpose:

Passion and purpose are the driving forces behind successful execution. Being deeply connected to the idea and understanding the underlying problem it aims to solve fuels determination and inspires others to join the journey. Passion ignites the fire that propels one forward, even in the face of adversity.

To execute with passion, it is essential to remain focused and committed. Avoiding distractions, staying organized, and maintaining a positive mindset are crucial to maintaining momentum. Celebrating small wins along the way reinforces motivation and helps to preserve energy for the challenges that lie ahead.

Learning and Adapting:

The path from idea to action is not a linear one. It is marked by uncertainties and unexpected obstacles. Iteration and adaptation are fundamental to success. Paying close attention to feedback and being open to change allows for continuous improvement.

Learning from mistakes and past experiences is equally important. Treat setbacks as opportunities to gain insights, adjust strategies, and pivot if necessary. Maintaining a growth mindset fosters a culture of innovation, ensuring constant evolution towards the desired outcome.

Chapter 4 has explored the transformative journey from idea to action. Beginning with the birth of an idea, we have discussed the importance of evaluation and refinement. We then delved into the dreamer's dilemma and the mindset required to overcome doubts and fears.

Developing an action plan, building a support network, executing with passion and purpose, and learning and adapting have been identified as crucial steps in the process. Although this chapter is but a snapshot of the arduous process of bringing ideas to life, it serves as a guide for aspiring creators, entrepreneurs, and innovators.

It is important to remember that every idea has the potential for greatness, but it is the application of action that truly makes a difference. So, as we move forward on our individual paths, let us embrace the challenges, persist with unwavering determination, and ultimately transform our ideas into reality.

Ideation and Market Research

In today's rapidly evolving business landscape, the success of any venture relies on the ability to identify innovative ideas and meet the demands of the target market. To achieve this, entrepreneurs and organizations must engage in a structured process of ideation and market research. This crucial phase lays the foundation for developing a compelling product or service that meets the needs of the consumers. In this chapter, we will explore the importance of ideation and market research and delve into the various techniques and methodologies employed to identify and validate potential business ideas.

Section 1: The Power of Ideation

1.1 Defining Ideation

Ideation is the process of generating, developing, and evaluating new ideas. It is the initial step in the journey of bringing a concept to life and transforming it into a tangible product or service. Ideation involves a creative and systematic approach to brainstorming, problem-solving, and identifying opportunities for innovation. By emphasizing the generation of novel ideas, ideation acts as a catalyst for entrepreneurship and fosters a culture of innovation within an organization.

1.2 The Role of Ideation in Entrepreneurship

Ideation is the lifeblood of entrepreneurship. It fuels the entrepreneurial spirit by encouraging individuals to challenge the status quo, identify gaps in the market, and develop unique solutions. Successful entrepreneurs are those who can think outside the box and spot opportunities where others might not see them. Ideation provides the necessary platform to initiate this process and lay the groundwork for the development of a viable business concept.

1.3 Techniques for Effective Ideation

a) Brainstorming: One of the most popular ideation techniques, brainstorming involves generating a large number of ideas, without any form of judgment or evaluation. By encouraging free-flowing ideas, individuals or teams can explore a wide range of possibilities and uncover hidden opportunities.

b) Mind Mapping: A visual technique that allows the generation of ideas by utilizing the brain's natural process of association. Mind mapping involves drawing a central idea and branching out into connected concepts, providing a holistic view of the problem space and fostering creativity.

c) SCAMPER: An acronym for Substitute, Combine, Adapt, Modify, Put to Another Use, Eliminate, and Reverse, SCAMPER is a versatile ideation technique that involves systematically challenging an existing idea by asking specific questions. By examining each element of the idea, entrepreneurs can identify opportunities for improvement and innovation.

d) Design Thinking: A human-centered approach that places the needs and desires of users at the forefront of the ideation process. Design thinking emphasizes empathy, experimentation, and iteration, promoting the development of solutions that truly resonate with the target audience.

Section 2: The Significance of Market Research

2.1 Understanding Market Research

Market research is the process of gathering, analyzing, and interpreting data about the target market to gain insights into consumer behavior, preferences, and market trends. It provides entrepreneurs with a deep understanding of the competitive landscape, enabling them to make informed decisions and develop strategies that maximize the chances of success.

2.2 The Importance of Market Research

a) Identifying Market Opportunities: Market research helps entrepreneurs identify unmet needs in the market, opening up opportunities for new product or service development. By analyzing consumer behavior and market trends, entrepreneurs gain a comprehensive understanding of the current demand and can adapt their offerings accordingly.

b) Mitigating Risks: By conducting market research, entrepreneurs can assess the viability and potential of their ideas before investing significant time and resources. This reduces the risk of failure and helps in avoiding costly mistakes that could have been avoided through proper market analysis.

c) Defining Target Audience: Market research aids in defining the target audience by segmenting the market based on demographics, psychographics, and other relevant factors. This segmentation allows entrepreneurs to tailor their offerings to cater to specific consumer needs and preferences, increasing the likelihood of success.

2.3 Market Research Methods

a) Surveys and Questionnaires: These traditional methods involve collecting data through structured questionnaires to gather insights into consumer preferences, opinions, and buying behavior. Surveys can be conducted through various channels, such as online platforms, email campaigns, or telephone interviews.
b) Focus Groups: Focus groups involve gathering a small group of individuals who represent the target audience. Through moderated discussions and interactive activities, entrepreneurs can gain qualitative insights, understand consumer perceptions, and identify emerging trends.
c) Interviews: One-on-one interviews with potential consumers or

industry experts provide entrepreneurs with in-depth insights, allowing them to understand pain points, motivations, and expectations from a more personal perspective.

d) Observational Research: This method involves directly observing consumers in their natural environment, assessing their behavior, preferences, and interactions with products or services. Ethnographic research and mystery shopping are examples of observational research techniques.

e) Data Analytics: With the rise of online platforms and digital marketing, entrepreneurs have access to vast amounts of data that can be mined and analyzed. Leveraging data analytics tools can provide valuable insights into consumer behavior, allowing entrepreneurs to make data-driven decisions.

Ideation and market research are essential steps in the entrepreneurial journey, facilitating the development of innovative products and services that cater to the needs of the target audience. By adopting structured ideation techniques and conducting thorough market research, entrepreneurs can mitigate risks, identify opportunities, and lay a strong foundation for future success. The careful blend of creative thinking and analytical insights gained from market research sets the stage for product development, marketing strategy, and ultimately, the growth and sustainability of a business.

Designing and Creating Your Digital Offerings

In today's digital era, creating compelling and innovative digital offerings is crucial for businesses to thrive and stand out in the highly competitive marketplace. As the demand for online products and services continues to soar, it becomes imperative for companies to design and create digital offerings that captivate their target audience and provide value. This chapter delves into the intricacies of developing and designing digital offerings, exploring key aspects such as user-centered design, effective content creation, seamless user experiences, and the importance of agile development.

User-Centered Design:

When it comes to designing digital offerings, adopting a user-centered approach is paramount. A user-centered design focuses on the preferences, needs, and goals of your target audience. By understanding your users' motivations and specific pain points, you can create digital offerings that resonate with them on a deeper level.

To adopt a user-centered design methodology, it is essential to conduct thorough user research. This research may involve surveys, focus groups, interviews, and analytics to gain insights into user behavior, preferences, and expectations. The data collected through this process will guide your design decisions and help you create a user experience tailored to your audience's needs.

Content Creation:

Creating engaging and valuable content is a critical element that sets successful digital offerings apart. Your content should not only be relevant but also captivating, informative, and compelling. It should provide users with the information they seek while reinforcing your brand identity and values.

One crucial aspect of content creation is understanding your target audience's preferences and the platforms they frequent. By knowing which channels your audience prefers, you can optimize your content creation strategy to generate maximum impact. Whether it's through blog posts, social media content, videos, or podcasts, align your content creation efforts with your audience's preferred media.

Moreover, it is important to focus on quality rather than quantity. Crafting well-researched, original, and insightful content will establish your brand as an authority in your industry and help build a loyal following. Remember, relevance and value are the cornerstones of effective content creation.

Seamless User Experiences:

A seamless user experience is crucial for the success of your digital offerings. Users should find it effortless to navigate through your website, app, or platform while achieving their desired goals. To accomplish this, always prioritize simplicity, clarity, and intuitive design.

Creating a consistent and visually appealing interface is vital for ensuring a seamless user experience. Choose a clear and logical layout, intuitive navigation menus, and visually pleasing aesthetics that reflect your brand identity. Additionally, optimize your offerings for different devices and screen sizes to accommodate the diversity of your audience.

Focus on Visual Design:

Visual design plays a significant role in attracting and engaging users. Well-chosen color palettes, typography, and imagery can significantly enhance the aesthetic appeal of your digital offerings. However, it is essential to strike the right balance between visual richness and simplicity.

Ensure that your content is presented in a visually pleasing manner, with clear and legible fonts, high-quality visuals, and proper spacing. Utilize colors that complement your brand and evoke the desired emotional response from users. Additionally, aim for consistency in design elements across your digital offerings to establish a recognizable and cohesive visual identity.

Agile Development:

Agile development methodologies have gained popularity in recent years due to their efficiency and adaptability. In the context of digital offerings, adopting an agile approach allows businesses to respond effectively to market changes and user feedback, resulting in continuous improvement and innovation.

Agile development emphasizes flexibility, collaboration, and iterative improvement. Rather than following a predefined, linear development process, it encourages ongoing feedback, frequent iterations, and the ability to respond swiftly to new requirements or insights. Prioritizing rapid prototyping, testing, and refining your digital offerings based on real-time user feedback can greatly increase their overall success and market acceptance.

Designing and creating digital offerings that captivate users and provide value is a complex yet crucial task in today's digital landscape. By adopting a user-centered design approach, focusing on content creation, ensuring seamless user experiences, and embracing agile development methodologies, businesses can leverage the power of digital technology to create offerings that resonate with their target audience and drive success.

With the continuous evolution of technology and changing user expectations, it is imperative for businesses to approach their digital offerings with a growth mindset. By constantly evaluating and refining their offerings, companies can keep pace with the ever-changing digital landscape, stand out from competitors, and build long-lasting customer relationships.

Platform Selection and Tech Essentials

In today's rapidly evolving technological landscape, the selection of a suitable platform is crucial for the success of any digital project. Whether you are a business owner or a software developer, understanding the key factors that drive platform selection is essential. This chapter will delve into the significance of platform selection and discuss some of the essential technologies that underpin modern digital solutions.

Why Platform Selection Matters:

When embarking on a digital project, one of the first crucial decisions is to choose the right platform. A platform can be defined as the underlying framework or infrastructure that supports and enables the operation of software applications. The selection of an appropriate platform can significantly impact the performance, scalability, security, and overall success of a project.

One of the primary aspects to consider when selecting a platform is the specific requirements of the project. Different projects have varying needs, such as high scalability for e-commerce platforms or robust security measures for financial systems. Understanding the project's requirements is essential to ensure the platform aligns with those needs.

Another critical factor to consider during platform selection is the target audience or user base. Different platforms cater to different demographics, and choosing a platform that resonates well with the intended audience can greatly enhance user engagement and adoption. For example, mobile applications are more suitable for platforms with a large percentage of mobile users, while web applications may be better suited for desktop users.

Platform Compatibility:

Compatibility is another crucial aspect that cannot be overlooked during platform selection. It is essential to ensure that the chosen platform is compatible with the existing infrastructure and technology stack. For example, if an organization has already invested heavily in Microsoft technologies, it may be more practical to select a platform that integrates seamlessly with these existing systems.

Scalability and Flexibility:

Scalability is a vital consideration when selecting a platform, especially for projects with potential growth and increased user traffic in the future. The platform should have the ability to scale up or down effortlessly, depending on the project's evolving needs. Additionally, a flexible platform allows for customization and integration with third-party tools. This flexibility is essential to ensure the platform can adapt to future business requirements and technology advancements.

Security and Reliability:

Security is paramount in today's interconnected world, where data breaches and cyber-attacks are becoming increasingly sophisticated. When selecting a platform, it is crucial to ensure that it provides robust security features, such as encryption, multi-factor authentication, and regular security updates. Reliability is also a significant consideration, as any downtime or technical glitches can impact the user experience and potentially harm the business's credibility.

Common Platforms:

A plethora of platforms are available today, each with its strengths and weaknesses. Here, we will discuss some of the most popular platforms and their unique features:

1. Web platforms: Web-based applications are widely used as they provide universal access via a web browser. The primary advantage of web platforms is their cross-platform compatibility, allowing users to access the application regardless of their operating system. Well-known web platforms include WordPress, Drupal, and Joomla, which offer content management capabilities for websites.

2. Mobile platforms: With the proliferation of smartphones, mobile platforms are highly sought after. These platforms enable developers to build applications specifically designed for mobile devices, taking advantage of features like GPS, camera functionality, and push notifications. iOS (Apple) and Android (Google) are two dominant players in the mobile platform space.

3. Cloud platforms: Cloud computing has revolutionized the way organizations deploy and manage their infrastructure. Cloud platforms, such as Amazon Web Services (AWS) and Microsoft Azure, offer a range of services, including virtual machines, storage, and networking solutions. These platforms provide high scalability, flexibility, and cost-effectiveness compared to traditional on-premises infrastructure.

4. IoT platforms: With the rise of the Internet of Things (IoT), platforms that enable seamless integration and management of various IoT devices have gained popularity. IoT platforms, such as Google Cloud IoT, IBM Watson IoT, and AWS IoT, provide tools to connect, analyze, and monitor IoT devices, opening up new possibilities for smart homes, industrial automation, and smart city initiatives.

Essential Tech Components:

Alongside platform selection, understanding the essential technologies that underpin modern digital solutions is crucial. As technology continues to evolve rapidly, staying up-to-date with these essential components ensures the successful development and deployment of digital projects. Here, we will discuss some of the key tech essentials:

1. Programming languages: Programming languages serve as the foundation for developing software applications. Popular languages like JavaScript, Python, and Java offer robust frameworks, libraries, and tools supporting different types of projects. Choosing the right

programming language that aligns with the project's requirements and the skill set of the development team is crucial.

2. Databases: Efficient data storage and retrieval are imperative for most digital projects. Relational databases like MySQL and PostgreSQL offer strong consistency and structured storage, whereas NoSQL databases like MongoDB and Cassandra provide scalability and flexibility. Understanding the nature of the data and its interaction with the application is crucial in selecting an appropriate database technology.

3. Application Programming Interfaces (APIs): APIs enable communication and data exchange between various software systems. They allow developers to leverage external services or build custom integrations in their applications. Well-known APIs, such as Google Maps API and Twitter API, provide developers with access to a wide array of services and data.

4. Front-end frameworks: User experience is a critical aspect of any digital project, and front-end frameworks play a significant role in delivering intuitive and responsive interfaces. Frameworks like React, Angular, and Vue.js simplify the process of developing interactive and dynamic user interfaces, leveraging reusable components and efficient rendering mechanisms.

5. DevOps tools: DevOps has become an integral part of modern software development, ensuring continuous integration, deployment, and monitoring processes. Tools like Git for version control, Jenkins for continuous integration, Docker for containerization, and Kubernetes for orchestration enable efficient

collaboration and deployment pipelines.

6. Artificial Intelligence (AI) and Machine Learning (ML): AI and ML technologies are transforming various industries, from image recognition to natural language processing. Integrating AI and ML capabilities into digital projects can greatly enhance user experiences and decision-making processes. Frameworks like TensorFlow and PyTorch provide developers with the necessary tools and algorithms for building sophisticated AI models.

Platform selection and understanding the essential technologies are crucial steps in the development of any digital project. This chapter provided a comprehensive overview of the significance of platform selection, highlighting key factors such as requirements, compatibility, scalability, security, and reliability. Additionally, it discussed some of the most popular platforms, including web, mobile, cloud, and IoT platforms, and introduced essential tech components like programming languages, databases, APIs, front-end frameworks, DevOps tools, and AI/ML technologies. By carefully considering these factors and technologies, businesses and developers can make informed decisions that align with their project goals, leading to successful outcomes in the ever-evolving digital landscape.

Developing a Minimum Viable Product (MVP)

In the world of product development, organizations often face the challenge of building a product that meets customers' needs while minimizing the time, effort, and resources invested. In recent years, a concept called the Minimum Viable Product (MVP) has gained prominence as a way to address this challenge effectively. In this chapter, we will explore the concept of MVP, understand its significance, and delve into the process of developing an MVP.

Defining the Minimum Viable Product:

The Minimum Viable Product (MVP) can be understood as a version of a product that is developed with the bare minimum features required to attract early adopters and collect valuable feedback. The primary objective behind an MVP is to validate a product idea or concept with minimal investment. This allows organizations to assess the viability and market potential of their product while minimizing the risk of building a complete and potentially unsuccessful product.

Why MVP Matters:

In today's fast-paced and highly competitive market, releasing a fully developed product without any prior testing can be a risky venture.

By adopting an MVP approach, organizations gain several advantages:

1. Reduced Time-to-Market: Developing an MVP allows organizations to get a product out into the market faster. By focusing on the essential features, developers can accelerate the development process, minimizing the time spent on non-essential aspects.

2. Validation of Ideas: MVPs enable organizations to test their product hypotheses and validate their assumptions without committing extensive resources. Through early adopter feedback and user testing, valuable insights can be gained, helping refine and improve the product before investing more significant amounts into it.

3. Cost Efficiency: Building and launching an MVP reduces the upfront costs associated with product development. By incorporating only the core features, organizations optimize their use of resources, allowing them to make informed decisions about further investment in product development.

Developing an MVP: The Process

While the development of an MVP may vary depending on the organization and product, there are certain key steps involved in the process that can be followed as a guide:

1. Identify the Target Market and Users: The first step in developing an MVP is understanding the target market and identifying the specific users who will benefit from the product. It is crucial to have a clear understanding of the pain points your product aims to solve and how it will provide value to the end-users.

2. Define the Core Features: Once the target market and user requirements are established, it is essential to define the core features required to deliver value to the users. The focus should be on developing a stripped-down version of the product with minimal functionality that addresses the identified pain points effectively.

3. Create a Prototype: After defining the core features, it is necessary to create a functioning prototype that showcases the product's basic functionalities. The prototype should be a simple, usable representation of the final product, allowing users to provide feedback and offer suggestions for improvement.

4. Collect and Incorporate Feedback: The next step involves gathering feedback from early adopters and potential users. This can be done through user testing, surveys, or any other means of direct

communication. The feedback collected should be carefully analyzed and used to iterate and refine the product.

5. Refine and Iterate: Based on the feedback received, it is crucial to iterate and refine the product continuously. This process may involve adding new features, improving existing ones, or making changes based on user preferences. The goal is to enhance the product's value proposition while keeping it aligned with the target market's needs.

6. Validate Market Viability: Once the refined product has been developed, it is crucial to assess its market viability. This involves analyzing the user adoption rate, measuring key metrics such as user engagement and retention, and validating the potential for monetization. The insights gained from this validation process will guide further product development and investment decisions.

Case Study: Spotify's MVP Journey

To illustrate the MVP concept in action, let's take a look at the journey of one of the most successful music streaming platforms: Spotify.

When Spotify first entered the market, it faced formidable competitors like iTunes and Pandora. To carve a niche for themselves, Spotify adopted the MVP approach. Their initial product offered one core feature: unlimited streaming of music in exchange for ad-supported usage. This stripped-down version allowed them to test their hypothesis that users would be willing to stream music freely in return for accepting ads. This MVP approach not only validated their concept but also provided valuable market insights. Based on user feedback, Spotify continuously refined its offerings. They introduced paid subscription plans, removed ads for premium subscribers, and implemented robust recommendation algorithms that learned from user preferences. Each iteration was built on the core idea validated through their MVP, leading to the robust platform we know today.

The concept of developing a Minimum Viable Product (MVP) has revolutionized the way organizations approach product development. By embracing the MVP mindset, companies can reduce time-to-market, validate their ideas, and optimize costs. The iterative process of MVP development allows organizations to gather user feedback, refine their product, and make informed decisions about future investments.

In this chapter, we explored the significance of MVPs, discussed the steps involved in the development process, and examined a real-world case study to emphasize the practical application of the concept. With MVPs being widely adopted across industries, organizations can now navigate the competitive market with greater confidence, knowing they have developed a product that is aligned with their target users' needs and preferences.

Chapter 5: The Art of Crafting Compelling Content

In today's digital age, where information is at our fingertips, the art of crafting compelling content has taken on a whole new level of importance. Whether you are a blogger, a marketer, or an aspiring novelist, your success often hinges upon your ability to captivate your audience with words. This chapter will delve into the techniques, principles, and strategies that can help you create content that leaves a lasting impact on your readers. So, grab your pen or fire up your keyboard, because we are about to embark on a journey to master the art of crafting compelling content.

The Power of Storytelling:

At the heart of compelling content lies the power of storytelling. People have always been enthralled by stories, whether passed down through generations or showcased on the silver screen. Storytelling is a fundamental aspect of human communication, and it creates an emotional connection between the storyteller and the audience. To craft compelling content, you must harness the power of storytelling to engage your readers on a deeper level.

The first step in storytelling is to understand your audience. What are their desires, fears, and aspirations? What questions are they seeking answers to? By empathizing with your audience, you can create content that resonates with them and speaks to their needs. It is essential to remember that compelling content is not just about you as the writer; it is about your readers and what they can gain from your words.

Crafting Captivating:

The introduction of any piece of writing is a make-or-break moment. It is your chance to hook your readers and entice them to keep reading. To create a captivating introduction, consider starting with a surprising fact, a thought-provoking question, or an intriguing anecdote. You need to grab your readers' attention from the very beginning and make them curious about what lies ahead. Clearly state the purpose of your content and promise to deliver value to your readers. Remember, first impressions matter, so make your introduction compelling enough to warrant further exploration.

Building a Solid Structure:

A compelling piece of content requires a solid structure. Without it, your thoughts may become disjointed, and your readers may struggle to follow your message. Begin by outlining the main points you want to cover and organizing them in a logical and coherent manner. This will help you maintain a clear focus and ensure that your content flows seamlessly from beginning to end.

Furthermore, your content's structure should be skimmable, allowing readers to find key information easily. Use headings, subheadings, and bullet points to break up your text and highlight important ideas. Remember that many readers tend to scan content rather than reading it word-for-word, so make it easy for them to find what they need.

The Power of Emotion:

Compelling content taps into emotions. It is the emotional connection that keeps readers engaged and invested in your words. When crafting your content, think about the emotions you want to evoke. Do you want your readers to feel inspired, motivated, or enlightened? Consider using sensory language, evocative imagery, and relatable stories to appeal to their emotions. Personal anecdotes, when used effectively, can create a sense of authenticity and allow readers to connect with you on a deeper level.

Effectively Using The Right Tone and Voice:

The tone and voice you adopt in your writing are crucial in establishing a connection with your readers. Whether you aim for an authoritative, friendly, conversational, or persuasive tone, it all depends on the purpose of your content and the relationship you want to build with your audience. Understanding your readers' preferences and requirements is key to adopting the right tone and voice.

Furthermore, consider incorporating your personality into your writing. Let your unique voice shine through, making your content distinctive and memorable. Readers appreciate authenticity, so don't be afraid to inject a dash of humor, personality, or vulnerability into your words.

Crafting Compelling Headlines and Subheadings:

Your content's headline and subheadings are the gateways to your article or blog post. Powerful headlines attract attention and entice readers to click on your content, while effective subheadings break up the text and provide readers with an overview of what to expect. When crafting headlines, aim for a combination of intrigue, clarity, and relevance. Experiment with different styles, such as using questions or employing action words, to see what works best for your audience.

Moreover, subheadings should be informative yet concise. They should serve as signposts, guiding your readers through your content and allowing them to skim for specific information. As with headlines, make your subheadings compelling enough to encourage continued reading.

The Importance of Research and Verifiability:

Compelling content requires a solid foundation of research and verifiability. Supporting your claims and arguments with credible sources not only enhances your content's credibility but also provides readers with the confidence to engage with your material. Incorporating statistics, studies, and expert opinions gives your content depth and authority. However, remember to fact-check your information and cite your sources properly to ensure accuracy.

Injecting Creativity and Innovation:

While facts and data may provide the basis for your content, injecting creativity and innovation can make it truly compelling. Avoid being mundane and predictable; instead, strive to bring fresh insights and perspectives to your writing. Experiment with different formats, such as infographics, videos, or interactive elements, to capture your audience's attention and make your content stand out from the crowd. Be bold, take risks, and challenge conventional wisdom. It is often through daring creativity that compelling content is born.

Crafting compelling content is not an easy task, but with practice and a deep understanding of your audience, you can become a master at it. By harnessing the power of storytelling, creating captivating introductions, building a solid structure, evoking emotions, adopting the right tone and voice, crafting compelling headlines and subheadings, conducting thorough research, and injecting creativity and innovation, you can create content that inspires, informs, and leaves a lasting impact on your readers.

Remember, the art of crafting compelling content is an ongoing journey of discovery and refinement. As you continue to hone your skills, you will unlock the ability to engage, motivate, and captivate your audience with your words. So, go forth, armed with the knowledge and principles outlined in this chapter, and let your creativity soar as you create extraordinary content that leaves a lasting impression.

Content Creation Strategies and Storytelling

In today's fast-paced digital era, content creation has become an integral part of any successful brand or business. To captivate and engage their audience effectively, content creators must employ well-thought-out strategies and harness the power of storytelling. In this chapter, we will delve into various content creation strategies and explore the art of storytelling, unraveling its significance and providing you with practical tips to enhance your content creation skills.

Understanding Content Creation:

Before we dive into the strategies and the magic of storytelling, it is essential to establish a foundational understanding of content creation itself. Content creation refers to the process of crafting and curating engaging and informative material, such as articles, videos, blogs, or social media posts, with the aim of captivating an audience and fostering a meaningful connection with them.

With the vast amount of content available online, the challenge lies in creating unique, valuable, and memorable content that effectively communicates your message. Several key elements can contribute to successful content creation strategies, including relevance, authenticity, creativity, and the ability to resonate with the target audience.

Crafting a Content Strategy:

To ensure that your content creation efforts yield optimal results, it is crucial to develop a well-defined content strategy. A content strategy acts as a roadmap, guiding you through the process of creating and distributing content that aligns with your overall business objectives. Let's explore a few key components of an effective content strategy:

1. Understanding your Target Audience: To create content that resonates with your audience, it is essential to have a clear understanding of their preferences, needs, and pain points. Conduct thorough market research, analyze data, and engage with your audience to gather insights that will inform your content creation decisions.

2. Choose the Right Platform: Different platforms cater to distinct target demographics and require unique content formats. Tailor your content to suit the platform you are using – whether it be blog posts, videos, social media posts, or podcasts – and adapt your messaging and style accordingly.

3. Consistency is Key: Building a loyal audience requires consistency in delivering high-quality content. Establish a content calendar to

ensure a regular flow of content and maintain a consistent brand voice that is aligned with your brand identity.

Harnessing the Power of Storytelling:

Storytelling serves as a means to connect with your audience on a deeper emotional level. A compelling story has the power to captivate and engage, evoking genuine emotions and provoking thought. Here are some key principles to consider when incorporating storytelling into your content creation:

1. Develop a Narrative Arc: A compelling story captures the attention of the audience by following a narrative structure. Beginning with an introduction or setup, followed by rising action, climax, falling action, and resolution, a comprehensive narrative arc helps keep your audience engaged till the end.

2. Understand the Hero's Journey: The Hero's Journey is a storytelling framework that revolves around the protagonist's transformation through challenges and growth. By incorporating this framework into your content, you can create relatable and inspiring narratives that resonate with your audience.

3. Emotions and Empathy: Stories that evoke powerful emotions have lasting impacts. Tap into the emotions of your audience using storytelling techniques such as building suspense, humor, or heartwarming moments. Additionally, infusing empathy into your

narratives helps establish a genuine connection with your audience by showing understanding and relatability.

4. Use Authenticity: Authentic stories that reflect genuine experiences and emotions hold more weight in the minds and hearts of your audience. Humanize your brand by sharing real stories and experiences that your target audience can relate to.

5. Visual Storytelling: Visuals play a significant role in conveying narratives effectively. Utilize imagery, videos, infographics, and other visually appealing assets to enhance storytelling and engage your audience in a more immersive way.

In this chapter, we explored the art of content creation strategies and storytelling. By crafting a well-defined content strategy that aligns with your business objectives and understanding your target audience, you can create engaging content that resonates with your intended audience. Additionally, storytelling helps establish a connection on an emotional level, immersing your audience in a captivating narrative experience. By incorporating these strategies and techniques into your content creation endeavors, you will be well-equipped to create compelling and impactful content that leaves a lasting impression on your audience. Remember, the power of storytelling lies within you, waiting to be unleashed.

Blogging and Article Writing for Beginners

In today's digital age, blogging has become an integral part of our lives. It has emerged as a powerful tool for expressing thoughts, sharing knowledge, building communities, and even making money. If you have ever contemplated starting a blog or writing articles, you have come to the right place. This chapter aims to provide beginners with a comprehensive guide to get started with blogging and article writing.

Section 1: Understanding Blogging and Its Potential

Before delving into the nuts and bolts of blogging, it is essential to comprehend the concept and possibilities it holds. A blog is a regularly updated online platform where writers share their insights, ideas, experiences, or expertise on specific topics. It allows individuals to present their unique perspectives, connect with like-minded people, and create an engaging conversation.

Blogs come in various forms, such as personal blogs, niche blogs, corporate blogs, or even journalistic blogs. While personal blogs reveal personal anecdotes, niche blogs focus on specialized subjects like fashion, travel, technology, or cooking, catering to a specific audience. Corporate blogs serve as marketing tools for companies, creating a powerful avenue for communication with clients and stakeholders. Journalistic blogs, on the other hand, cover current events and often provide opinions or analysis.

The potential of a blog is immense. It can help shape your personal brand, establish you as an authority in your field, or even generate income through various monetization methods, such as advertising, sponsored content, or affiliate marketing. It is a platform that enables you to express your creativity, share your knowledge, and build a loyal readership.

Section 2: Choosing a Blogging Platform

Choosing the right blogging platform is crucial for a successful start. Several popular platforms offer user-friendly interfaces, customizable designs, and reliable hosting services. The most commonly used platforms are WordPress, Blogger, and Medium.

WordPress stands as the most prevalent choice, powering over 30% of all websites on the internet. It offers a self-hosted option, wherein you obtain greater control over your blog's design and functionality. However, setting up a self-hosted WordPress blog requires purchasing a domain name and a hosting plan.

Blogger, owned by Google, is an easy-to-use platform with free hosting. It offers a simple interface and a range of customizable templates, making it beginner-friendly. While it has limited customization options compared to WordPress, it provides a hassle-free way to start blogging, particularly for personal or hobby blogs.

Medium is a platform designed for writers, covering a wide range of topics. It allows you to focus solely on writing without worrying about technical aspects, as Medium handles the hosting and design. However, it offers limited customization options and fewer opportunities for monetization.

Section 3: Identifying Your Niche and Target Audience

Once you have chosen a blogging platform, it is essential to identify your niche and determine your target audience. A niche is a specialized topic or subject that your blog will be centered around. Identifying a niche helps you establish your authority and attract a dedicated readership.

To zero in on your niche, consider your interests, passions, and areas of expertise. Think about what you enjoy writing or talking about the most. It could be anything from travel, health, technology, or finance. By focusing on a specific niche, you can create content that caters to a particular audience, increasing your chances of building a loyal following.

Understanding your target audience is equally important. Research and analyze the demographics, interests, and preferences of your potential readers. This knowledge will guide your content creation process, enabling you to produce relevant, valuable, and engaging articles or blog posts that resonate with your audience.

Section 4: Creating Engaging and Valuable Content

The backbone of a successful blog or article lies in creating attractive, informative, and valuable content. Here are a few tips to help you produce engaging content:

1. Catchy Headlines: Craft attention-grabbing headlines that compel readers to click and read your content. A compelling headline is concise, clear, and promises value or solution.

2. Storytelling: Weave storytelling elements into your articles to captivate readers. Engaging narratives make your content relatable and emotionally appealing.

3. Clear Structure: Organize your writing using headings, subheadings, and bullet points. This helps readers comprehend your content and locate specific information easily.

4. Research and Credibility: Back your claims and statements with supporting evidence from trustworthy sources. Research your topics thoroughly to provide credible information to your audience.
5. Authenticity and Personal Touch: Inject your unique voice and personality into your writing. This creates a genuine connection with your readers and distinguishes your work from others.

6. Visual Content: Incorporate relevant images, infographics, or videos to complement your text. Visual content enhances the overall appeal of your blog posts or articles.

Section 5: Optimizing Your Blog for Search Engines

Search engine optimization (SEO) is crucial to ensure your blog or articles rank higher in search engine results. Here are a few essential SEO tips:

1. Keyword Research: Identify and use relevant keywords that your target audience is likely to search for. Keyword research tools can help you uncover popular search terms within your niche.

2. On-Page SEO: Optimize your content by including keywords in the blog post title, headings, Meta description, and naturally throughout the article. Also, ensure your URLs are concise and descriptive.

3. Quality Backlinks: Build quality backlinks to your blog by guest posting on other authoritative websites or by leveraging your network. Backlinks from reputable sources enhance your blog's credibility and visibility.

4. Responsive Design: Ensure your blog or website is mobile-friendly, as an increasing number of users access content from their smartphones or tablets. Search engines prioritize mobile-friendly sites in their rankings.

Section 6: Engaging with Your Readers and Building a Community

Successful blogging involves more than just creating content; it requires actively engaging with your readers and building a loyal community. Here are some effective ways to engage your audience:

1. Respond to Comments: Encourage readers to leave comments and respond to them promptly. Engaging in meaningful conversations with your readers builds a sense of community and loyalty.

2. Consistency: Publish content regularly to keep your readers' interest alive. Develop a consistent schedule, whether it's weekly, bi-weekly, or monthly, and stick to it.

3. Social Media Presence: Leverage social media platforms to promote your blog and reach a wider audience. Share your blog posts, interact with your followers, and actively participate in relevant communities or groups.

4. Email Newsletter: Start building an email list to stay connected with your readers and offer exclusive content or updates. Email newsletters are an effective way to nurture relationships and drive traffic to your blog.

Section 7: Monetizing Your Blog

If you have aspirations to monetize your blog and earn income, there are several avenues to explore. Here are a few popular methods:

1. Advertising: Displaying ads on your blog through programs like Google AdSense can generate revenue based on clicks or impressions.

2. Sponsored Content: Collaborate with brands or companies to produce sponsored content. This involves featuring their products or services in your blog posts or articles for a fee.

3. Affiliate Marketing: Promoting products or services through affiliate links can earn you a commission for every sale generated through your referral.

4. Digital Products: Create and sell your own digital products, such as e-books, courses, or templates, catering to your target audience's needs.

5. Coaching or Consulting: If you establish yourself as an expert within your niche, you may offer coaching or consulting services to your readers or clients.

Section 8: Continuous Learning and Growth

Finally, blogging is a continuous learning process. Stay updated with the latest trends, writing techniques, and tools in the industry. Read other blogs, attend webinars, or join forums to network and exchange ideas with fellow bloggers.

Experiment with different writing styles and content formats to keep your blog engaging and fresh. Stay open to feedback, adapt to changes, and continue honing your writing skills to ensure your blog's continuous growth and success.

Blogging and article writing offer an incredible opportunity to express yourself, share knowledge, and engage with a wide audience. By choosing the right platform, understanding your niche, creating engaging content, optimizing for search engines, building a community, and exploring monetization options, you can embark on a fascinating journey as a blogger. Remember, success in the world of blogging is built on consistency, passion, authenticity, and continuous learning. So, what are you waiting for? Start your blogging adventure today!

Creating Engaging Visual and Video Content

In today's digital era, where attention spans are diminishing and competition for eyeballs is fierce, creating visually captivating content has become an essential skill for marketers, creators, and businesses alike. Harnessing the power of compelling visual and video content can not only captivate your audience but also increase brand awareness, drive traffic, and ultimately boost conversion rates. This chapter will delve into the art and science of creating engaging visual and video content and highlight essential strategies and techniques to make your content stand out from the crowd.

1. Understanding the Importance of Visual and Video Content

Visual content plays a pivotal role in capturing and retaining the attention of your target audience. According to a survey conducted by HubSpot, 54% of consumers prefer video content from the brands they support, indicating the dominance of visual mediums. This preference arises from our inherent inclination towards consuming information in a visually engaging format, as well as the ability of visuals to convey emotions, tell stories, and simplify complex ideas.

2. Leveraging the Power of Storytelling in Visual Content

Storytelling is a timeless tool that has been used for centuries to captivate audiences. When it comes to visual and video content creation, storytelling becomes even more crucial. By incorporating narratives and emotions into your visuals, you can create a deeper connection with your viewers. Whether you're sharing a customer success story, documenting behind-the-scenes moments, or presenting a compelling brand narrative, storytelling adds depth and meaning to your content, making it more memorable and impactful.

3. Design Principles for Compelling Visuals

To create visually captivating content, understanding the principles of design can prove invaluable. Here are some key principles to guide your visual content creation process:

a) Composition: The arrangement of elements within an image determines how visually pleasing and balanced it appears. Experiment with framing, rule of thirds, leading lines, and negative space to create visually appealing compositions.

b) Color Psychology: Colors evoke emotions and can influence the way your audience perceives your content. Research color theory to leverage the psychological effects of different hues in your visuals. For example, warm tones like orange and red can evoke feelings of excitement and urgency, while blues and greens can evoke calmness and trust.

c) Typography: Font choices and text placement are essential when incorporating text into your visuals. Ensure that the typography aligns with your brand identity, remains legible, and complements the overall composition of the image.

d) Consistency: Consistency across your visual content builds brand recognition and trust. Establish a cohesive visual style by adhering to a clear color palette, font selection, and image treatment. Consistency helps reinforce your brand identity and makes your content instantly recognizable.

4. The Power of Video Content

Videos have become an indispensable part of any content strategy due to their immense engagement potential. Whether it's short-form videos for social media platforms or long-form videos for tutorials or storytelling, adopting a video-first approach can yield significant benefits for your brand. Here are a few strategies to create impactful video content:

a) Choose the Right Platform: Different platforms have varying video formats and durations. Tailor your content to fit the platform's requirements and leverage its unique features. For instance, 15-second vertical videos perform exceptionally well on platforms like TikTok and Instagram Reels.

b) Create High-Quality Content: Quality matters when it comes to video content. Invest in good equipment, ensure proper lighting, and use professional editing software to enhance the visual appeal of your videos. Poor video quality can deter viewers and diminish the impact of your message.

c) Incorporate Storytelling and Emotion: As mentioned earlier, storytelling adds depth and emotion to your visuals. Use narrative arcs, relatable characters, and interesting visuals to immerse viewers in your story. Emotional storytelling triggers empathy and resonates better with your audience.

d) Optimize for Mobile: With the increasing dominance of mobile devices, optimizing your videos for mobile viewing has become essential. Ensure that your video maintains its visual appeal, remains legible on smaller screens, and loads quickly even with limited bandwidth.

5. Tools and Techniques for Visual and Video Content Creation
Creating engaging visual and video content doesn't require a professional studio or a massive budget. Numerous tools and techniques are readily available to help you get started. Here are a few popular ones to consider:

a) Canva: Canva is an intuitive graphic design tool that allows you to create stunning visuals, social media graphics, and videos using customizable templates, an extensive library of assets, and easy-to-use editing features.

b) Adobe Creative Cloud: Adobe's suite of professional tools, including Photoshop, Illustrator, and Premiere Pro, offers unparalleled creative possibilities for visual content creation. These tools provide advanced editing capabilities for professionals seeking to take their content to the next level.

c) User-Generated Content: Encouraging your audience to generate content for you can be a powerful way to enhance engagement. Create photo or video contests, use branded hashtags, or share user-generated content to leverage the creativity of your customers and strengthen your brand's authenticity.

d) Animation Tools: Animation adds an extra layer of engagement to your visuals. Tools like Powtoon, Vyond, or Adobe After Effects allow you to create animated explainer videos or visually appealing motion graphics without requiring extensive design or coding knowledge.

By harnessing the principles of design, embracing storytelling, leveraging video content, and utilizing the plethora of tools available, you can create visually captivating and engaging content that resonates with your audience. Remember, with the digital landscape constantly evolving, it's essential to stay on top of current trends and continuously experiment with new techniques to keep your content fresh and captivating. So, go forth, unleash your creativity, and create visually stunning content that leaves a lasting impression on your viewers.

Podcasting as a Tool for Audience Building

In the digital age, where content consumption has become increasingly mobile and on-demand, podcasts have emerged as a powerful medium for connecting with audiences. With the ability to reach listeners anytime and anywhere, podcasting has transformed the way individuals and businesses communicate, educate, and entertain. This chapter delves into the world of podcasting as a tool for building a loyal and engaged audience. We will explore the history of podcasting, its popularity, benefits, and the strategies for successfully leveraging this medium to connect with listeners.

The Rise of Podcasting:

Podcasting, a portmanteau of "iPod" and "broadcasting," first emerged in the early 2000s, coinciding with the rise of portable media players. This audio-based content delivery method allowed users to download and listen to episodes of their favorite shows at their convenience. Initially, podcasting was a niche market, mainly fueled by dedicated tech enthusiasts, but it quickly gained traction as major media players recognized its potential.

Apple's entry into the podcasting sphere with iTunes in 2005 played a crucial role in propelling it into the mainstream. This move made it extremely accessible, allowing users to discover, subscribe to, and automatically download episodes effortlessly. As a result, the number of podcasts grew exponentially, covering diverse topics ranging from news and personal development to comedy and storytelling.

The Popularity of Podcasting:

The unprecedented growth of podcasting is a testament to its popularity among users as well as content creators. According to recent studies, over 50% of the US population has listened to a podcast, and over 32% of Americans listen to podcasts at least monthly.

One of the key factors driving the popularity of podcasts is their inherent convenience. Unlike other mediums, podcasts offer a hands-free and eyes-free experience, making them perfect for listening during commutes, workouts, or while doing household chores. Moreover, the long-form nature of podcasts fosters deep engagement, allowing hosts to build personal connections and establish credibility with their listeners.

Benefits of Podcasting:

1. Enhanced Engagement: By offering immersive and long-form content, podcasting fosters a sense of connection and intimacy with the audience. The intimate nature of audio can create stronger

engagement and loyalty compared to other media formats.

2. Extended Reach: Podcasts have the potential to reach a global audience. With virtually no geographical boundaries, podcasts enable individuals and businesses to connect with listeners from different backgrounds, cultures, and demographics.

3. Niche Targeting: Podcasts make it easy to target specific niches and cater to specialized interests. Unlike traditional radio or television, where content needs to appeal to a mass audience, podcasts thrive on their ability to serve passionate communities.

4. Cross-promotion Opportunities: Podcasting allows for cross-platform promotion, amplifying your presence across various channels. Whether it's referencing your podcast on social media or directing listeners to your website, podcasts serve as an effective hub for promoting other content and offerings.

5. Monetization Possibilities: Podcasts offer numerous monetization opportunities, ranging from sponsorships and advertising to merchandise sales and crowdfunding. With a growing listener base, podcasts can become a revenue stream for content creators.

Strategies for Successful Audience Building:

1. Define Your Target Audience: Before diving into podcasting, it's crucial to identify and understand your ideal listeners. Create listener personas that encompass their demographic details,

interests, and pain points. By tailoring your content to resonate with this group, you can cultivate a loyal following.

2. Unique Value Proposition: To stand out amongst the plethora of podcasts available, you must offer a unique value proposition. Determine how your podcast differentiates itself—whether through subject matter, approach, or format—and ensure it resonates with your target audience.

3. Consistency and Frequency: Consistency is key in building a loyal audience. Set a regular publishing schedule and stick to it. Whether it's weekly, bi-weekly, or monthly, providing fresh content at predictable intervals keeps listeners engaged and eager for more.

4. Quality Production: While content is king, high-quality production values contribute to the overall listening experience. Invest in good audio equipment, edit episodes meticulously, and maintain sound clarity. Attention to production details reflects your commitment to delivering a professional podcast.

5. Engaging Hosting Style: A compelling host can make or break a podcast. Develop a hosting style that resonates with your target audience. Be authentic, empathetic, and conversational. Engage the listeners through storytelling, interviews, and thought-provoking discussions.

6. Leveraging Guest Appearances: Inviting guests to your podcast not

only diversifies the content but also exposes your podcast to wider audiences. Collaborate with experts, influencers, or industry leaders to attract their followers while adding value to your podcast.

7. Promote, Promote, Promote: Developing exceptional content is only the first step. Effective promotion is vital in reaching a broader audience. Leverage social media, email marketing, and your website to create buzz around your podcast. Cross-promote with other podcasts or relevant platforms to tap into new listener bases.

8. Engage with Your Community: Foster an active and engaged community around your podcast. Encourage listeners to interact through comments, emails, or social media discussions. Responding to feedback and incorporating listener suggestions not only deepens connections but also adds value to your content.
Podcasting has emerged as a powerful tool for audience building and engagement in an increasingly digital world. Its popularity, convenience, and ability to forge meaningful connections have made it a crucial medium for individuals and businesses looking to reach and resonate with their target audiences. By leveraging the strategies outlined in this chapter, content creators can successfully navigate the podcasting landscape and build a loyal and engaged listener base.

Chapter 6: Igniting Your Online Presence

In today's digital age, having a strong online presence is not only a luxury but a necessity for individuals and businesses alike. Whether you are a budding entrepreneur, an established professional, or someone looking to make a name for themselves, the internet offers unparalleled opportunities to showcase your talents, connect with a global audience, and propel your career to new heights. This chapter will explore the key strategies and essential elements to ignite your online presence and make a lasting impact in the virtual world.

1. Crafting Your Digital Identity:

Before setting out to establish your online presence, it is crucial to define your digital identity. This entails determining who you are, what you represent, and the message you want to convey to your target audience. Take the time to introspect and understand your values, passions, and unique selling points. Reflect on what sets you apart from others in your niche and how you can leverage those strengths to build a personal brand that resonates with your audience.

2. Building an Engaging Website:

A website is the cornerstone of your online presence, serving as your virtual headquarters. It provides an opportunity to showcase your portfolio, display your work, share your ideas, and establish yourself as an authority in your field. Ensure that your website is visually appealing, user-friendly, and easily navigable. Incorporate engaging content, including a compelling bio, a portfolio of your work, testimonials from satisfied clients or customers, and a blog section to share valuable insights with your audience.

3. Optimizing for Search Engines:

In a world where millions of websites are vying for attention, search engine optimization (SEO) is paramount. Implementing effective SEO techniques will improve your website's visibility in search engine results pages, driving organic traffic to your site. Conduct thorough keyword research to identify relevant terms that your target audience would search for. Incorporate these keywords naturally into your website's content, headings, meta tags, and URLs to improve your ranking.

4. Harnessing the Power of Social Media:

Social media platforms have revolutionized the way we connect, communicate, and build online relationships. Leveraging social media effectively can significantly enhance your online presence.

Identify the platforms that align with your industry and target audience and establish a thoughtful presence on them. Regularly share engaging content, interact with your followers, and utilize features like hashtags, polls, and live videos to boost engagement and attract a larger audience.

5. Content Creation and Marketing:

Compelling content lies at the heart of an impactful online presence. Create high-quality and valuable content that resonates with your target audience, showcases your expertise, and solves their problems. This could include blog posts, articles, videos, infographics, podcasts, or even interactive tools. Develop a content strategy that focuses on providing consistent and useful information your audience craves while staying true to your brand's voice and tone.

6. Engaging with Online Communities:

Active participation in online communities can offer a plethora of opportunities to expand your reach, establish credibility, and connect with like-minded individuals. Seek out relevant forums, groups, or communities on platforms like Reddit, Quora, or LinkedIn where you can contribute valuable insights, answer questions, and engage in meaningful discussions. By adding value to the community, you will naturally attract attention and stimulate interest in your online presence.

7. Seeking Influencer Collaborations:

Collaborating with influential individuals or brands can serve as a powerful catalyst to ignite your online presence. Identify key influencers in your industry whose audience aligns with your target market. Reach out to them with tailored proposals to collaborate on projects, guest blogs, interviews, or joint ventures. By associating yourself with established figures, you can leverage their credibility and tap into their audience, enhancing your online visibility.

8. Online Advertising and Marketing:

While organic methods are effective for building an online presence, investing in targeted online advertising can offer a significant boost. Platforms like Google AdWords, Facebook Ads, or Instagram Ads allow you to reach a broader audience and target specific demographics. Develop a comprehensive advertising strategy that aligns with your goals, budget, and target audience to maximize the return on your investment.

9. Monitoring and Engaging with Feedback:

To flourish in the online realm, it is essential to monitor and promptly respond to feedback from your audience. Encourage your audience to leave comments, reviews, or testimonials and engage with them openly and respectfully. Address any concerns or criticisms professionally and take them as opportunities to learn, grow, and fine-tune your online presence continuously. Your willingness to listen and adapt will demonstrate your commitment to fostering genuine connections with your audience.

10. Tracking and Analyzing Metrics:

Lastly, regularly evaluate and analyze the performance of your online presence to optimize your strategies and achieve better results. Utilize web analytics tools like Google Analytics to track key metrics such as website traffic, click-through rates, engagement levels, and conversion rates. This data will provide insights into which strategies are working effectively and those that need refinement, enabling you to adapt and refine your approach accordingly.

Embrace the Digital Revolution:

In today's interconnected world, your online presence holds immense potential to propel your personal and professional growth. By crafting a compelling digital identity, creating engaging content, utilizing social media platforms effectively, and embracing online marketing strategies, you can ignite your online presence and achieve remarkable success. Embrace the opportunities that the digital revolution presents and position yourself for an exciting future where the virtual world becomes the gateway to real-life opportunities.

Building and Optimizing Your Business Website

In today's digital era, a business website is more than just a virtual storefront; it's a powerful tool that can drive growth, increase brand visibility, and boost customer engagement. However, creating an effective website requires careful planning, strategic execution, and continuous optimization.

In this chapter, we will explore the essential steps involved in building and optimizing a business website that captivates your target audience, ranks well in search engines, and converts visitors into loyal customers. From defining your website's goals to implementing SEO techniques, we will cover everything you need to know to create a successful online presence.

Setting Goals and Objectives

Before diving into the technical aspects of website development, it is crucial to define your goals and objectives. Think about what you aim to achieve with your website. Are you looking to generate leads, sell products/services, or establish your brand as an industry leader? Clearly outlining your goals will provide a roadmap for the entire website-building process.

User-Centric Design

A visually appealing and user-centric design is the foundation of a successful website. User experience plays a pivotal role in keeping visitors engaged and converting them into customers. When designing your website, consider the following aspects:

1. Responsive Design: With the increasing use of mobile devices, it is essential to have a responsive design that adapts to different screen sizes. This ensures a seamless experience for all users.

2. Intuitive Navigation: Make sure your website has clear and easy-to-use navigation. Users should be able to locate information effortlessly, reducing the risk of them leaving your site in frustration.

3. Eye-Catching Visuals: Use high-quality images and videos to make your website visually appealing. However, strike a balance between aesthetics and page loading speed, as slow-loading content can be a turnoff for visitors.

Compelling Content

"Content is king" is a common phrase in the digital marketing world, and for a good reason. Engaging and informative content not only attracts visitors but also keeps them coming back. Consider the following approaches to create compelling content for your website:
1. Thoroughly Research Your Target Audience: Understanding your

target audience's interests, pain points, and search habits will help you create content that speaks directly to them.

2. Incorporate SEO Best Practices: When crafting content, keep search engine optimization (SEO) in mind. Conduct keyword research, optimize meta tags and headings, and create informative and shareable content.

3. Utilize Various Content Formats: Mix different content formats such as blog posts, videos, infographics, and podcasts to cater to different audience preferences. This diversification allows you to engage with a broader audience base.

Search Engine Optimization (SEO)

Optimizing your website for search engines is crucial to increase its visibility organically. Here are a few key areas to focus on when implementing SEO:

1. Keyword Optimization: Conduct thorough keyword research and incorporate relevant keywords naturally throughout your website, including in page titles, meta descriptions, headers, and content.

2. Link Building: Establishing strong backlinks from high-quality and authoritative websites is vital for search engine rankings. Seek opportunities to guest post, collaborate with influencers, or create shareable content that naturally attracts backlinks.

3. Site Speed and Performance: A slow-loading website can significantly impact your search rankings. Optimize your website's speed by compressing images, minifying code, and leveraging caching mechanisms.

Conversion Optimization

While attracting visitors to your website is important, converting them into customers is the ultimate goal. Here are some strategies to optimize your website's conversion rate:

1. Clear and Compelling Calls-to-Action (CTAs): Strategically place CTAs throughout your website to guide visitors towards desired actions. Make them visually appealing, clear, and persuasive.

2. Simplify the Conversion Process: Reduce friction by streamlining the conversion process. Minimize the number of form fields, optimize the checkout process, and offer guest checkout options.

3. Leverage Social Proof: Display customer testimonials, reviews, case studies, and social media shares to build trust with your visitors. Social proof provides reassurance and encourages visitors to take action.

Monitoring and Continuous Improvement

Building a website is an ongoing process that requires continuous monitoring and improvements. Use analytics tools like Google Analytics to track user behavior, measure key performance indicators (KPIs), and identify areas for enhancement. Regularly analyze the data and make data-driven improvements to optimize your website further for better results.

Building and optimizing your business website is an essential aspect of establishing a strong online presence. By setting clear goals, designing with the user in mind, and incorporating compelling content, your website can serve as a valuable tool for attracting and converting customers. Furthermore, implementing effective SEO techniques and continuously monitoring and improving your website will ensure its long-term success. Remember, your website is a direct reflection of your brand, so invest time and effort into creating an exceptional online experience for your target audience.

The Magic of Email Marketing Campaigns

In today's digital landscape, email marketing has emerged as a powerful tool for businesses to connect with their target audience. With its ability to reach a vast number of individuals instantaneously, email marketing campaigns have become an essential component of any successful marketing strategy. In this chapter, we will explore the various aspects that make email marketing campaigns magical and how they can help businesses unlock their true potential.

Building and Growing Your Email List:

The foundation of a successful email marketing campaign lies in a well-curated email list. As a business, it is crucial to create opportunities for potential customers to subscribe to your emails voluntarily. One effective way to achieve this is by offering valuable content in exchange for their email addresses. This could include e-books, exclusive discounts, or newsletters packed with insightful industry information.

It is essential to remember that building a quality email list is more important than merely increasing its size. A targeted email list consisting of individuals who have shown genuine interest in your brand or industry ensures a higher engagement rate and better conversion numbers.

Designing Engaging Email Campaigns:

Once you have a solid email list, the next step is to design visually appealing and engaging email campaigns. Email templates provide a foundation for crafting compelling messages that align with your brand's aesthetics. Personalization is an essential factor in increasing the effectiveness of your campaigns, as recipients are more likely to engage with content that feels tailored specifically to them.

Using segmentation is another powerful technique in designing engaging email campaigns. By dividing your email list into smaller segments based on demographics or preferences, you can effectively target your audience with more personalized content. This increases the likelihood of recipients opening your emails and converting into customers.

Key Elements of an Email Campaign:

To create a magical email marketing campaign, it is essential to understand the key elements that make it successful. Firstly, a strong subject line that grabs the reader's attention is crucial for increasing open rates. It should be concise, relevant, and evoke curiosity without appearing spammy or misleading.
The body of the email should be well-crafted, concise, and visually

appealing. Utilize active language, persuasive copy, and compelling visuals to capture the reader's interest and drive them towards the desired action, which could be making a purchase, signing up for a webinar, or simply visiting your website.

Incorporating a clear Call-to-Action (CTA) within your email campaign is vital. The CTA should be prominently displayed and strategically placed to guide the reader towards taking the desired action. Including social sharing buttons within your email content also encourages recipients to share your email with their networks, extending your reach and potentially attracting new subscribers.

Driving Engagement and Building Relationships:
Email marketing campaigns not only allow businesses to promote their products or services but also provide opportunities to foster relationships with their subscribers. Regularly sharing valuable content, such as industry insights or how-to guides, establishes your brand as a reputable source of information and builds trust with your audience.
Interactive elements, such as surveys, quizzes, or contests, can also be included in your email campaigns to encourage engagement and gather valuable customer feedback. Taking the time to engage with your subscribers by responding to their queries or concerns also goes a long way in building a loyal customer base.

Tracking and Analyzing Campaign Performance:

To fully harness the magic of email marketing campaigns, it is crucial to track and analyze their performance. Email marketing platforms offer various metrics and analytics tools to help you measure the success of your campaigns. Open rates, click-through rates, and conversion rates provide valuable insights into how recipients are engaging with your emails.

By analyzing these metrics, you can identify trends, understand what elements of your campaigns are resonating with your audience, and make data-driven decisions to optimize future campaigns for even better results. A/B testing different subject lines, email designs, or CTAs can further refine your approach and improve the effectiveness of your campaigns.

Effective Email Marketing Practices:

While email marketing campaigns hold immense potential, it is important to follow some best practices to ensure their success. Firstly, send relevant and timely emails by understanding your audience's preferences and behaviors. Bombarding subscribers with irrelevant content can lead to higher unsubscribe rates and a negative perception of your brand.

Also, remember to optimize your emails for different devices, as a considerable portion of readers access their emails on mobile devices. Ensuring mobile responsiveness and concise, scannable content will enhance the user experience and increase the likelihood of engagement.

Leveraging Influencer Collaborations

In today's digital age, social media has revolutionized the way we connect, communicate, and consume information. With billions of users across various platforms, the influence of social media is undeniable. As a result, marketers have leveraged this phenomenon to enhance their brand's reach and engage with their target audience. One of the most effective strategies in this realm is collaborating with influencers. In this chapter, we will explore the world of influencer collaborations, discussing their significance, benefits, potential pitfalls, and how to maximize their impact on your brand.

6.1 Understanding Influencer Marketing

Before diving into influencer collaborations, it is crucial to grasp the concept of influencer marketing. Influencer marketing involves partnering with individuals who have a substantial following on social media platforms. These individuals, known as influencers, have established their credibility and authority within specific niches or industries.

Gone are the days of relying solely on traditional advertising methods. Consumers today are more likely to trust the opinions and recommendations of those they admire or relate to. Therefore, influencer marketing has become an indispensable tool for brands to connect with their target audience authentically.

6.2 The Power of Influencer Collaborations

Leveraging influencer collaborations can yield numerous advantages for brands. Let's explore some of the most compelling reasons why influencer collaborations have become such an effective marketing strategy.

6.2.1 Expanded Reach and Enhanced Engagement

The primary advantage of influencer collaborations lies in the ability to tap into the vast following of influencers. These individuals have spent considerable time and effort building their audience, fostering relationships, and establishing trust. When brands collaborate with influencers whose audience aligns with their target demographic, they gain direct access to a highly engaged and relevant audience.

Through influencer collaborations, brands can extend their reach far beyond their existing customer base. They can effectively fuel brand awareness and generate buzz about their products or services. By partnering with influencers, brands can leverage their credibility to enhance engagement and encourage consumers to interact with their brand.

6.2.2 Authentic and Trustworthy Recommendations

One of the most potent aspects of influencer collaborations is their ability to provide authentic and trustworthy recommendations. Influencers have earned the trust of their audience by consistently delivering high-quality content and establishing themselves as experts in their field.

When influencers genuinely endorse a brand or product, their followers are more likely to perceive it as a credible recommendation rather than an explicit advertisement. Leveraging influencer collaborations allows brands to tap into this credibility, leading to increased trust and a higher chance of consumers trying and advocating for their products or services.

6.2.3 Content Creation and Diversification

Another significant advantage of influencer collaborations lies in the abundance of user-generated content. Influencers are skilled content creators who understand the preferences and interests of their audience. When brands collaborate with influencers, they gain access to a vast reservoir of tailored content that can be repurposed across various channels.

From captivating photos and engaging videos to informative blog posts and compelling testimonials, collaborations with influencers allow brands to create diverse and captivating content. This multifaceted approach not only enriches brand storytelling but also helps maintain a fresh and dynamic online presence.

Online Networking and Community Engagement

In the digital age, the internet has transformed the way we connect and engage with others. Online networking platforms have become a powerful tool for individuals and communities to establish connections, form meaningful relationships, and foster engagement. This chapter explores the vast landscape of online networking and community engagement, delving into its benefits, challenges, and the ways in which it has reshaped the world as we know it.

1. The Rise of Online Networking Platforms

With the advent of the internet, networking has transcended physical boundaries and evolved into a global phenomenon. Online networking platforms such as Facebook, LinkedIn, Twitter, and Instagram have become household names, offering users the ability to connect with others, share information, and participate in vibrant virtual communities.

These platforms have become instrumental in connecting individuals across the globe, breaking down barriers of distance, language, and culture. They bring people together in ways that were inconceivable just a few decades ago, allowing us to create and nurture relationships with like-minded individuals, regardless of geographical constraints.

2. Enhancing Professional Networking

One of the most significant advantages of online networking platforms is their ability to facilitate professional connections. LinkedIn, in particular, has emerged as a paramount platform for professionals, enabling them to showcase their skills, experience, and accomplishments. It serves as a virtual resumé, providing a comprehensive overview of an individual's career trajectory.

The platform also supports the establishment of professional communities, allowing individuals to connect with others in their field, seek mentorship, and engage in fruitful discussions. These networks provide opportunities for career growth, job searches, and staying up-to-date with industry trends.

3. Building Supportive Communities

Beyond professional spheres, online networking platforms have birthed a plethora of communities united by diverse interests, passions, and hobbies. For instance, Facebook groups have become a hub for people with shared interests to come together, discuss their passions, seek advice, and offer support.

From cooking enthusiasts to book clubs, fitness aficionados to pet lovers, there is a community for almost every interest imaginable. These spaces foster a sense of belonging, enabling individuals to connect with others who share their enthusiasm, collaborate on projects, and expand their knowledge.

4. Crowdsourcing and Collaborative Initiatives

The rise of online networking has also revolutionized how collective endeavors are undertaken. Crowdsourcing has become a valuable resource for gathering ideas, feedback, and financial support from a large pool of contributors.

Platforms like Kickstarter, GoFundMe, and Patreon have paved the way for creators, entrepreneurs, and artists to obtain support from a global audience. This collaborative approach has democratized innovation by providing opportunities for anyone with a compelling idea to turn it into reality with the backing of virtual communities.

5. Challenges and Risks of Online Networking

While online networking presents numerous benefits, it is essential to acknowledge and address the challenges and risks that come with it. One predominant challenge is the issue of privacy and security. As we willingly share personal details and engage with others online, there is a risk of identity theft, fraud, and cyberbullying.

Furthermore, the ubiquity of social media has led to the spread of misinformation and fake news. The ease of sharing information on online platforms has created an environment in which false narratives can quickly gain traction, leading to widespread confusion and discord.

6. Maintaining Authenticity and Meaningful Connections

As online networking continues to evolve, it is crucial to preserve the authenticity and depth of our connections. The digital realm can often create a facade, leading to superficial interactions and a sense of disconnection from reality. Striking a balance between online engagement and meaningful face-to-face interactions is essential for maintaining a healthy social life.

7. Leveraging Online Networking for Social Change

Perhaps one of the most significant impacts of online networking has been its ability to amplify voices and catalyze social change. Movements like #MeToo and Black Lives Matter gained traction and mobilized millions across the globe through the power of online communities.

Online platforms have provided marginalized communities a platform to share their experiences, mobilize support, and challenge the status quo. Activists and social change makers can now connect, organize, and collaborate on a global scale, fostering a collective voice that demands justice and equality.

8. The Future of Online Networking

As technology continues to evolve, so too will the landscape of online networking. The integration of virtual reality (VR) and augmented reality (AR) is expected to provide an immersive and innovative experience, allowing users to connect in new and exciting ways. Additionally, artificial intelligence (AI) will play a fundamental role in enhancing online networking platforms. AI algorithms will become more adept at matching individuals based on their interests, establishing deeper connections and fostering more meaningful relationships.

The possibilities are endless, and the future of online networking holds tremendous potential for positive change, increased connectivity, and community engagement.

Online networking platforms have become an integral part of our lives and have transformed the way we connect, engage, and collaborate. From enhancing professional networks to fostering supportive communities and amplifying voices for social change, these platforms continue to reshape the world we live in.

Nevertheless, it is vital to navigate this digital realm mindfully, being aware of the risks and challenges that come hand in hand with the abundance of opportunities and connections online networking provides.

Chapter 7: Navigating the E-Commerce Landscape

In today's digital age, the e-commerce landscape is evolving at an astonishing rate. As technology continues to advance, businesses face new challenges and opportunities in establishing their online presence. Chapter 7 of this book delves into the intricacies of navigating the ever-changing e-commerce landscape, providing insights and strategies to thrive in this dynamic environment.

Understanding the E-Commerce Revolution

The rise of e-commerce has revolutionized the way businesses operate and consumers shop. Gone are the days of solely brick-and-mortar stores; online platforms have become a crucial channel for companies to reach their target audience. As a result, understanding the fundamentals of e-commerce is paramount for success in the modern business landscape.

In this chapter, we will explore the key elements that shape the e-commerce landscape and elucidate the strategies necessary for navigating it effectively. We will discuss the importance of user experience, online marketing, effective logistics management, and the integration of emerging technologies.

The Power of User Experience

User experience (UX) plays a pivotal role in the success of any e-commerce venture. Offering an intuitive and seamless customer experience is imperative to attract and retain consumers. Chapter 7 delves into the core pillars of exceptional UX and provides practical advice on how to optimize websites and mobile applications for maximum customer satisfaction.

Furthermore, the chapter explores the significance of personalized experiences, the role of artificial intelligence in enhancing UX, and the utilization of user data analytics to drive targeted marketing campaigns. By understanding and implementing these strategies, businesses can forge deeper connections with their customers and foster long-term loyalty.

Online Marketing Strategies for E-Commerce Success

In an increasingly crowded e-commerce landscape, effective marketing strategies are essential for businesses to stand out from the competition. Chapter 7 delves into the various online marketing channels available to e-commerce entrepreneurs, offering insights on how to leverage search engine optimization (SEO), social media marketing, content marketing, and influencer partnerships to drive traffic and increase conversions.

Moreover, the chapter explores the power of email marketing

campaigns, the benefits of affiliate marketing programs, and the potential of pay-per-click (PPC) advertising. By employing a comprehensive and integrated marketing approach, businesses can reach their target audience effectively and increase their return on investment.

Optimizing Logistics and Fulfillment

Behind every successful e-commerce operation lies an efficient logistics and fulfillment system. Ensuring a seamless customer experience from click to delivery is crucial to building a reputable online brand. Chapter 7 dives into the complexities of logistics management, providing entrepreneurs with a blueprint for optimizing inventory management, order fulfillment, and shipping processes.

Additionally, the chapter dissects the emergence of third-party logistics providers, the benefits of dropshipping, and explores how advanced technologies such as drones and robotics are reshaping the shipping landscape. By implementing streamlined logistics practices, businesses can enhance their operational efficiency and deliver exceptional customer experiences.

Embracing Emerging Technologies

The e-commerce landscape is ever-evolving, and staying ahead of the curve requires a willingness to embrace emerging technologies. In

Chapter 7, we explore the transformative potential of technologies such as virtual reality (VR), augmented reality (AR), and the Internet of Things (IoT) in shaping the future of e-commerce.

By harnessing VR and AR technologies, businesses can provide immersive shopping experiences to their customers, allowing them to visualize products virtually. Furthermore, the chapter discusses the immense potential of IoT, enabling businesses to collect and analyze data that can drive personalized marketing strategies. Embracing these technologies positions businesses at the forefront of the e-commerce landscape and propels them towards sustainable growth.

Chapter 7 serves as a comprehensive guide to navigate the e-commerce landscape successfully. By understanding the importance of user experience, implementing effective marketing strategies, optimizing logistics, and embracing emerging technologies, businesses can position themselves for long-term success in an ever-evolving digital world.

Although this chapter merely scratches the surface of the myriad concepts and strategies pivotal to e-commerce success, it provides a solid foundation for entrepreneurs and businesses seeking to flourish in the online marketplace. By continually adapting and innovating, businesses can thrive in the e-commerce landscape and embrace the limitless opportunities it holds.

Choosing the Right E-Commerce Model

In this digital era, the world has witnessed a revolutionary shift towards online shopping and e-commerce. With millions of consumers embracing the convenience and accessibility of online platforms, businesses have recognized the immense potential of e-commerce in expanding their customer base and increasing revenue. However, for entrepreneurs and business owners, the challenge lies in choosing the right e-commerce model that aligns with their goals, resources, and target audience. In this chapter, we will explore various e-commerce models and provide insights to help you make an informed decision.

1. Business-to-Customer (B2C) Model:

The Business-to-Customer model, commonly known as B2C, is the most recognizable e-commerce model. It involves transactions between businesses and individual consumers. B2C e-commerce platforms, such as Amazon and eBay, have gained widespread popularity due to their seamless user experience, vast product range, and personalized recommendations. This model is ideal for businesses targeting a large consumer market, as it enables direct interaction with end-users and provides valuable insights for marketing and customer relationship management.

2. Business-to-Business (B2B) Model:

As the name suggests, the Business-to-Business model focuses on transactions between businesses. B2B e-commerce platforms facilitate sales of goods or services between companies, such as manufacturers, wholesalers, and retailers. This model streamlines the procurement process by offering features like bulk purchasing, negotiated pricing, and integrated supply chain management systems. B2B e-commerce has gained prominence in industries such as manufacturing, healthcare, and construction, where large-scale purchases and strategic partnerships are common.

3. Consumer-to-Consumer (C2C) Model:

The Consumer-to-Consumer e-commerce model enables individuals to engage in online transactions with each other, eliminating the need for intermediaries. Platforms like Craigslist and Etsy provide spaces where users can buy and sell goods directly with other consumers. C2C e-commerce has flourished due to the rise of social media and peer-to-peer communication, allowing individuals to tap into the online marketplace by leveraging their own resources and expertise. This model is particularly popular in the second-hand market, creative handcrafted goods, and the sharing economy.

4. Consumer-to-Business (C2B) Model:

Traditionally, businesses sell products or services to consumers. However, the Consumer-to-Business e-commerce model reverses this relationship, enabling individuals to offer their goods or services to businesses. Freelancing platforms like Upwork and Fiverr are examples of C2B models, where individuals can showcase their skills and expertise and businesses can hire them for specific projects or services. This model is gaining traction as the gig economy and remote work become increasingly prevalent, allowing businesses to tap into a pool of freelance talent.

5. Peer-to-Peer (P2P) Model:

The Peer-to-Peer model is a subset of the C2C model, where individuals can connect and transact directly with each other without relying on a centralized platform. This decentralized nature of P2P e-commerce removes intermediaries and reduces transaction costs. An exemplary illustration of this model is cryptocurrency platforms, such as Bitcoin, which enable individuals to exchange digital assets without the involvement of banks or financial institutions. P2P e-commerce models are not limited to digital currencies; they are also found in areas such as car-sharing, home-sharing, and crowdfunded lending.

6. Subscription-Based Model:

The Subscription-Based e-commerce model has gained popularity in recent years, offering recurring services or product deliveries to customers. Companies like Netflix and Spotify thrive on this model, offering monthly or annual subscriptions for unlimited access to their digital content. Subscription-based models foster customer loyalty and provide a predictable revenue stream for businesses. This model is especially suitable for businesses offering digital content, software services, or products with frequent replenishment needs.

7. Dropshipping Model:

The Dropshipping model is an e-commerce fulfillment method where businesses do not physically stock the products they sell. Instead, they forward customer orders to a third-party supplier, who then ships the products directly to the customers. This model eliminates the burden of inventory management, warehousing, and fulfillment for businesses, making it an attractive option for entrepreneurs starting with limited resources. Dropshipping platforms like Shopify have made it easier than ever to set up an online store without the need for substantial upfront investment.

Considerations for Choosing an E-commerce Model:

When selecting the right e-commerce model for your business, several key factors should be taken into account:

1. Target Audience: Understand your target audience's preferences, online behavior, and purchasing habits. Ensure that the chosen e-commerce model aligns with their needs and expectations.

2. Scalability: Consider the scalability of your chosen model. Can it accommodate rapid growth and increasing customer demand without compromising quality and service?

3. Cost and Resources: Evaluate the financial implications and resources required to establish and maintain your chosen e-commerce model. Consider factors such as platform fees, marketing expenses, technology infrastructure, and manpower requirements.

4. Competitive Landscape: Analyze the competitive landscape within your industry and explore how different e-commerce models have been successful for similar businesses. Identify gaps or opportunities that can be leveraged with your chosen model.

5. Integration and Customization: Assess the compatibility of your chosen e-commerce model with existing systems and workflows. Ensure that it can be seamlessly integrated into your business processes and offers enough flexibility for customization.

6. Data Security and Privacy: As online transactions involve sensitive customer information, ensure that your chosen e-commerce model prioritizes data security and privacy. Comply with relevant regulations and industry best practices to protect your customers' trust.

Effective Product Photography and Descriptions

When it comes to selling products online, a picture is worth a thousand words. In the fast-paced digital marketplace, quality product photography and compelling descriptions can make or break a sale. Consumers rely heavily on visual cues to evaluate products, and it is crucial for businesses to showcase their offerings in the best possible light. In this chapter, we will explore the art of effective product photography and descriptions, uncovering techniques to captivate potential customers and drive sales.

1. The Power of Visuals

Visuals are one of the most influential factors in consumer decision-making, especially in the realm of e-commerce. In a physical store, customers have the luxury of examining products up close, touching and feeling them. However, in the online world, customers rely solely on visuals to make informed buying decisions. Effective product photography becomes the bridge between the customer's physical experience and the virtual world of online shopping.

2. The Role of Product Photography

Product photography is an art form that combines technical

expertise and creativity to capture a product's essence and convey its unique qualities. Product photos must accurately represent the item for sale, showcasing its features, dimensions, and appearance. Great product photography should strive to inspire trust and desire in potential customers, making them confident in their choice to purchase.

2.1 Equipment and Set-up

Investing in quality photography equipment is essential in capturing professional product images. A digital single-lens reflex (DSLR) camera with interchangeable lenses is a go-to choice for many photographers due to its versatility and high image quality. Additional equipment such as tripods, lighting kits, and reflectors can also enhance the overall outcome of product photography.

A well-designed set-up is crucial for achieving consistent and visually appealing product images. A clean, clutter-free background with complementary props can provide context and help customers envision the product in their own lives. It is paramount to ensure adequate lighting, as it plays a significant role in highlighting the product's features and enhancing its visual appeal.

2.2 Composition and Styling

Composition is the key to capturing attention and creating an engaging visual experience for potential customers. It involves arranging various elements within the frame, such as the product itself, props, and background, to create a visually pleasing image. The iconic rule of thirds is often employed to guide the placement of main elements in the frame, adding balance and interest.

Styling is an essential element in product photography, particularly for lifestyle products. Thoughtful arrangements of props and accessories can enhance the product's appeal, build an emotional connection with the customer, and showcase its potential uses. Skillful styling understands and reflects the target audience's desires, making them more likely to envision themselves using the product.

3. Importance of High-Quality Images

High-quality product images contribute significantly to a customer's perception of a product's value, quality, and desirability. In the competitive e-commerce landscape, where countless options are just a few clicks away, capturing attention and standing out is of utmost importance. Investing in high-quality images can have a tangible impact on sales conversion rates and customer satisfaction.

3.1 Resolution and Image Size

The resolution of product images should be high enough to allow customers to zoom in and examine details without pixelation or blurriness. Low-resolution images can make products appear unprofessional and undermine the perceived quality of the item.

Additionally, ensuring appropriate file sizes optimize website loading times, enhancing the overall user experience.

3.2 Multiple Angles and Detail Shots

Providing multiple angles and detail shots of a product allows customers to virtually inspect it from various perspectives. This helps build confidence in the product's features, authenticity, and overall quality. Detail shots showcase intricate workmanship, surface textures, and finer details that make the product unique, convincing customers of its value.

4. Crafting Compelling Product Descriptions

While product photography grabs initial attention, persuasive and informative descriptions complement the visual elements and provide essential details. Crafting compelling product descriptions requires a deep understanding of the product, its features, and its target audience. Here are some key aspects to consider when writing product descriptions:

4.1 Know Your Audience

Understanding your target audience is paramount when creating product descriptions that resonate with potential buyers. Research your customer demographics and identify their pain points, desires, and motivations. Tailor your language and tone to speak directly to this audience, using words and phrases that resonate with them on an emotional and intellectual level.

4.2 Highlight Features and Benefits

Incorporate key product features and benefits into the description to give customers a clear understanding of what the product offers and how it can enhance their lives. Focus on how the product solves a problem or fulfills a need, and highlight any unique selling points that differentiate it from competitors. This helps create a sense of value and urgency, encouraging customers to make a purchase.

4.3 Be Descriptive and Engaging

Use descriptive language that paints a vivid picture in the customer's mind. Instead of simply stating dimensions or materials, provide sensory details that allow customers to imagine using the product. Engage their emotions and senses by describing how the product feels, smells, or sounds, capturing their imagination and captivating their interest.

4.4 Utilize Social Proof and Testimonials

Incorporate social proof and customer testimonials into your product descriptions to strengthen your brand credibility and reinforce customers' trust. Highlight positive reviews or share stories of how your product has positively impacted your customers' lives. This can alleviate any doubts customers may have and give them the confidence to proceed with their purchase.

Effective product photography and descriptions play a vital role in driving online sales and influencing customer perceptions.

From capturing attention with high-quality images to crafting engaging and persuasive product descriptions, businesses must invest time, effort, and resources into perfecting this critical aspect of e-commerce.

By mastering the art of visual storytelling and appealing to customers' emotions and desires, businesses can create a powerful connection with potential buyers and drive their success in the competitive online marketplace.

Pricing Strategies for Online Success

Pricing is a critical aspect of any business strategy, and the online realm is no exception. The rise of e-commerce has significantly transformed the way consumers shop and engage with brands. With the vast ocean of online stores and cutthroat competition, businesses need to adopt effective pricing strategies to not only attract customers but also maximize profits. In this chapter, we will delve into seven pricing strategies that can help businesses succeed in the online world.

1. Competitive Pricing:

Competitive pricing is a strategy that involves setting product prices in line with or slightly below the average market price. The aim is to gain a competitive edge by offering customers a similar product at a more attractive price point. Online retailers can measure and monitor competitors' prices using sophisticated price tracking tools. By analyzing market trends and aligning prices accordingly, businesses can entice customers with appealing deals and maintain a competitive position in the market.

2. Psychological Pricing:

Psychological pricing is an age-old tactic that leverages human behavior and perception to influence buying decisions. Using pricing strategies such as charm pricing (ending prices in 9, 99, or 95), prestige pricing (presenting higher prices to convey superior quality), and bundle pricing (offering multiple products as a package at a discounted price), businesses can tap into consumers' subconscious desires and encourages them to make a purchase. This strategy works exceptionally well in the online realm, where customers are more inclined to seek out perceived discounts and value.

3. Dynamic Pricing:

Dynamic pricing refers to adjusting product prices based on real-time market demand, seasonality, customer insights, and competitive factors. This approach enables businesses to optimize profits by charging higher prices during peak demand periods or offering discounts to encourage sales during slow periods. Online retailers can leverage sophisticated algorithms and AI-driven pricing tools to automate dynamic pricing decisions. By actively monitoring market conditions, businesses can stay agile and maximize revenue based on ever-changing customer behavior.

4. Price Discrimination:

Price discrimination is a strategy that involves charging different prices for the same product or service based on various customer segments, such as demographics, geographic locations, or purchasing behavior. Online businesses have a wealth of customer data that can be analyzed to identify and target specific market segments. By tailoring prices to specific customer groups, businesses can achieve higher sales and profitability. However, companies should be cautious to avoid any unethical practices or sharp practices that may lead to negative reputation or legal implications.

5. Freemium Pricing:

Freemium pricing is widely used in the online world, especially in the software and digital content industries. This strategy involves offering a basic version of a product or service for free while charging a premium price for additional features or enhanced functionality. By allowing customers to experience the product before making a financial commitment, businesses can significantly increase user adoption and acquisition rates. Freemium pricing also creates opportunities for upselling and cross-selling, leading to long-term revenue growth.

6. Penetration Pricing:

Penetration pricing is a strategy typically employed by new entrants or businesses aiming to expand market share rapidly. It involves setting low initial prices to attract customers and gain a foothold in the market. Online businesses can take advantage of their lower operating costs compared to brick-and-mortar stores to offer competitive prices. As online sales volume increases, businesses can gradually adjust prices to more sustainable levels while still capturing a significant share of the market.

7. Value-Based Pricing:

Value-based pricing hinges on a deep understanding of customers' needs and their willingness to pay for a product or service. By positioning products as high-value solutions and effectively communicating the benefits to customers, businesses can set higher prices and generate a higher profit margin. To implement value-based pricing successfully, extensive market research, customer feedback analysis, and constant monitoring of customer preferences are essential. This strategy allows businesses to differentiate themselves based on the value they offer rather than solely competing on price.

Pricing strategies play a pivotal role in determining the success of online businesses. Whether it's adopting competitive pricing to stay ahead of the competition or leveraging psychological tactics to influence consumer behavior, online retailers must continually adapt their pricing strategies to thrive in the ever-evolving digital landscape.

By employing the right pricing strategies tailored to their target audience and business goals, online businesses can not only attract more customers but also increase profitability and achieve sustainable growth in the competitive online marketplace.